THE MILFORD SERIES
Popular Writers of Today

ISSN 0163-2469
Volume Thirty-six

From Here to Absurdity

The Moral Battlefields of Joseph Heller

by

Stephen W. Potts

R. Reginald

San Bernardino, California
MCMLXXII

W9-AJR-716

CONTENTS

Library of Congress Cataloging in Publication Data:

Potts, Stephen W., 1949-
    From here to absurdity.

    (The Milford series ; popular writers of today ; v. 36)
    Bibliography: p. 64.
    1.Heller, Joseph—Criticism and interpretation. I. Title. II. Series.
PS3558.E476Z83   813'.54   81-21602
ISBN 0-89370-156-4 (cloth, $9.95)   AACR2
ISBN 0-89370-256-0 (paper, $3.95)

Produced, designed, and published by R. Reginald and Mary A. Burgess, The Borgo Press, P.O. Box 2845, San Bernardino, CA 92406, USA. Cover design by Michael Pastucha.

First Edition————September, 1982

INTRODUCTION

Rare is the first novel successful enough to make its author's reputation. Rarer still is the work of fiction that actually adds a term to the language. Joseph Heller's *Catch-22*, published in 1961, did both.

Joseph Heller was born on May 1, 1923, in the Coney Island section of Brooklyn, New York, where all of Heller's public schooling took place. With the onset of American involvement in World War II, the young Heller became a blacksmith's helper at the Navy Yard in Norfolk, Virginia. He left to enter the Army as a Shipping File Clerk, then ultimately enlisted in the U.S. Air Force in October, 1942. He avoided becoming a gunner, having heard that the average life span of a gunner in combat was three days, by entering cadet school. After graduating with the rank of 1st Lieutenant in 1944, he saw combat as a bombardier in the skies over Italy.

Like most of his fellow novices, he found participation in the war fun at first. On his 37th mission, however, the co-pilot of his plane, fearing the B-25 was going to stall, panicked, grabbed the controls from the pilot, and took the plane into a steep dive. Heller found himself pressed to the ceiling of his bombardier's compartment in the nose, his headphones torn loose, helpless to act or to communicate with the rest of the crew. When the plane finally leveled off, allowing Heller to plug his headset back into the intercom, the first thing he heard was the voice of the co-pilot sobbing, "Help him! Help him!" "Help who?" Heller shouted into the mike. "Help the bombardier," the co-pilot replied. Heller experienced a deathly chill, but recovered quickly enough to rejoin, "*I'm* the bombardier. I'm all right." "Then help *him*," came the reply. Heller crawled into the rear of the plane to find the gunner wounded in the thigh. He decided then that that experience was as close as he wanted to come to death. It also provided the seed for his later masterpiece. Though he ended up flying a total of sixty missions, it was a wiser, more sober Lt. Heller who was discharged from active duty at the war's end.

Under the G.I. Bill, Heller headed for the University of Southern California to commence his undergraduate career, transferring shortly thereafter to New York University. While there, he found himself particularly impressed by the short story writing course taught by Maurice Baudin. His experience in the class convinced him of his aptitude for fiction. When he left NYU in 1948 with a B.A. in English and a Phi Beta Kappa key, he already had the first of his professional publications behind him.

His premiere in print was a short story that appeared in a special issue of *Story* magazine (Sept./Oct. 1945) devoted to the fiction of returning veterans. Lt. Heller's contribution was "I Don't Love You Any More," a simple, conventional piece about a young veteran who offends his wife by snidely asking for a pitcher of beer when she is begging him to dress for company; she walks out in anger, and the sobered young man greets their guests alone. As he escorts them out of the apartment, apologizing for having ruined the evening, his wife makes a surprise return—with the beer. Heller's other undergraduate sketches and stories appeared in *Atlantic* and *Esquire*, all in the then-standard vein of seedy naturalism, subtle irony, and cynical twist endings pioneered a decade earlier by the latter magazine. "Bookies, Beware!" (*Esquire*, May 1947), a silly one-page piece about a college student who "scientifically" picks a long shot to win a horse race, heads this list, followed by "Castle of Snow" (*Atlantic*, March 1948), a boy's reminiscence of his uncle's struggle to survive the depression: "Girl from Greenwich" (*Esquire*, June 1948), in which a man violently defends a woman from another man, only to discover that she was in the wrong; and two tales playing off the twisted morality of New York's petty criminal set—"A Man Named Flute" (*Atlantic*, August 1948), and "Nothing to Be Done" (*Esquire*, August 1948).

None of these stories brought Heller anything resembling the recognition, remuneration, or artistic satisfaction he expected, so he set aside the writing of fiction temporarily to continue his career in education. Following a 1949 Master's degree in English from Columbia University and a Fulbright Fellowship to Oxford, Heller became an instructor of English composition at Pennsylvania State University. In 1952 he abandoned academe for the private sector and a career in advertising, writing copy or doing promotion work for *Time*, *Look*, *McCall's*, and Remington Rand.

In the mid-fifties Heller began the writing of an ambitious full-length work rooted in his World War II experience, tentatively entitled *Catch-18*. The first chapter, named for the whole, appeared in *New World Writing No. 7* (New York, 1955). It is essentially identical to the first chapter of *Catch-22*, except for some additional dialogue and description later pared. Nothing in this excerpt, however, indicates that the completed novel would be any more than a showcase for servicemen's humor in the wacky Max Schulman manner.

Catch-18 was accepted for publication by Simon and Schuster in 1957 on the basis of the first few chapters. While Heller worked to complete the novel, he sold two more short stories in his imitative undergraduate style, "MacAdam's Log" (*Gentlemen's Quarterly*, December 1959), and "World Full of Great Cities" (*Nelson Algren's Book of Lonesome Monsters*, New York: Bernard Geis, 1963). The latter in particular, an episode concerning a teen-aged messenger boy who runs away from a decidedly seamy attempt at seduction, reflects the naturalistic, ironic mode in which *Esquire* had specialized.

Joseph Heller's authorial career really did not get under way until the 1961 publication of *Catch-22*, its title changed from *Catch-18* to avoid comparison with *Mila 18*, the then-latest novel of Leon Uris, popular author of *Exodus*. It was greeted with mixed reviews, ranging from Nelson Algren's remark, familiar to owners of the original edition, that this was the "best American novel to come out of World War II [and] . . . the best American novel that has come out of anywhere in years" (*The Nation*, 4 November 1961), to the comment of the reviewer for the literary magazine *Daedalus*, that *Catch-22* was "worthless."

The book took off slowly at first in the United States, though it hit the best seller lists in London upon its British release in 1962. A respectable but not particularly impressive 35,000 copies had been sold in the U.S. before the Dell paperback came out in the Fall of 1962. Only then did the novel hit its stride, with two million copies sold as of 1968. The book owed much of its success to its discovery by a generation angry about the escalating war in Vietnam and disillusioned in general with the military, government bureaucracy, capitalism, and the dissonance between the preachment and the practice of American ideals. *Catch-22* and the Sixties needed each other. It was a book whose time had come.

I: CATCH-22

On its surface, *Catch-22* is a novel about World War II, about the courageous cowardice of its anti-hero Yossarian, and about the stupidity and inequity of our institutions, particularly military institutions. The work, however, presents a number of problems to casual readers and critics alike. No one can get far past the first chapter without discovering the book's unusual and confusing narrative structure. Events taking place at sundry times and places are interconnected in an apparently random, free-associative sequence, and one often finds oneself yanked form one to another mid-paragraph, or even mid-sentence. It is difficult, in fact, to determine which events precede which. Critics have made meticulous attempts to unravel the chronology of the plot, some successfully, some not so.

Another difficulty is the profusion of characters, ranging from the sympathetic to the pathetic to the utterly detestable, from those who are central to the main plot and themes to those who receive mere occasional mention or who figure in sideplots of their own. Compounding the difficulty of keeping the characters straight is their generally cartoon-like, two-dimensional depiction, not to mention their overlapping and doubling. While the above obstacles to reader comprehension may be—indeed, have been—considered faults of the novel, they do serve artistic and thematic purposes.

In *Catch-22*, narrative structure, rhetorical technique, characters, and themes are bound—one could say "tangled"—so intricately that it is all but impossible to deal with each element separately. Fortunately, despite the complex time scheme, the novel does manifest a structural and thematic development of sorts. One can, for the purposes of analysis, divide the work into a number of broad divisions containing several chapters each, and more or less differentiated from one another in the events and characters dealt with, as well as in overall tone.

The first chapter of the novel, and thus the first division, begins in the hospital, where we are introduced to Yossarian through his first dialogue with the chaplain, to Yossarian's fake liver condition, which is untreatable because it falls short of being jaundice; to his whimsical censoring of letters under the name Washington Irving; and to the soldier in white—essentially an anonymous, humanoid shell of plaster and bandages—who quickly becomes the first casualty mentioned in the book. We also meet Dunbar, Yossarian's kindred spirit, who actively seeks boring and disagreeable situations in order to make his life seem longer. This chapter is relatively uneventful, and as noted earlier regarding its previous life as "Catch-18," it only dimly foreshadows the hilarity, absurdity, and morbidity to follow.

Here, however, Heller introduces the reader to a couple of rhetorical techniques that predominate in the first division, techniques that will have thematic significance later. One is apparent direct contradiction, or "oxymoron." For instance, early in the chapter we read: "The Texan turned out to be good-natured, generous and likable. In three days no one could stand him." Three pages later Yossarian tells the chaplain, " 'Nately had a bad start. He came from a good family,' " and further on describes Dunbar as " 'One of the finest, least dedicated men in the whole world.' " Another technique insistent throughout this first section is repetition, as for example in this exchange:

> "You're a chaplain," he exclaimed ecstatically. "I didn't know you were a chaplain."
> "Why, yes," the chaplain answered. "Didn't you know I was a chaplain?"
> "Why, no. I didn't know you were a chaplain." (p. 13. All page references are to the Dell edition.)

One early and anonymous reviewer complained that these two devices, what he referred to as "self-contradictory statements" and "echolalia," were the only two forms of ostensible wit in the entire novel (*Daedalus*, 92 [Winter 1963], pp. 155-165). Indeed, in the first few chapters they are so frequent as to appear redundant, particularly as attempts at humor. In Chapter Two, for example, a description of the character Appleby ends with the assertion "and everybody who knew him liked him." The very next line, however, is " 'I hate that son of a bitch,' Yossarian growled." This is followed a paragraph later by yet another sequence of echolalia:

> "That Yossarian," the two officers laughed, shaking their heads, and got another ball from the box on the shelf.
> "That Yossarian," Yossarian answered them.
> "Yossarian," Nately whispered cautioningly.
> "You see what I mean?" asked Clevinger.
> The officers laughed again when they heard Yossarian mimicking them. "That Yossarian," they said more loudly.
> "That Yossarian," Yossarian echoed.
> "Yossarian, please," Nately pleaded.
> "You see what I mean?" asked Clevinger. (p. 19)

Similar exchanges appear throughout the first section. Related to the practice of direct contradiction noted above is the multiple use of negatives, often with confusing or nonsensical results, from the relatively simple, "Orr rolled up the side flaps to allow a breeze that never blew to flush away the air baking inside" and "On the other side of Havermeyer stood the tent McWatt no longer shared with Clevinger, who had still not returned when Yossarian came out of the hospital," to the long description of the echolalic Major Major Major's Yankee father, heavily laced with such internally contradictory statements as "He was a proud and independent man who was opposed to unemployment insurance and never hesitated to whine, whimper, wheedle, and extort for as much as he could get from whomever he could." It is in such remarks that the relationship of this particular technique to the novel's themes becomes evident: Major Major's father is merely one of the many characters who represent the inherently contradictory nature of ideals in general, and the American practice of these ideals in particular. Beyond the satirical application of these techniques, however, lies a deeper purpose: in their contradictory, circular, and redundant nature, these devices lay in the first chapters the philosophical foundation for the novel's fictive universe—a world in which values mutually contradict and frequently cancel one another completely, in which men find themselves running in unending circles of impossible illogic.

At the heart of this thematic quantum lies "Catch-22" itself, first mentioned at length in Chapter Five. In a discussion between Yossarian and the self-pitying surgeon, Doc Daneeka, Yossarian tries to get himself grounded by reason of insanity. The doctor replies, however, that if Yossarian really *wants* to be grounded, he is therefore sane and must continue to fly missions, since "a concern for one's own safety in the face of dangers that were real and immediate was the process of a rational mind." The paragraph goes on to explain that Yossarian's tentmate

> Orr was crazy and could be grounded. All he had to do was ask; and as soon as he did, he would no longer be crazy and would have to fly more missions. Orr would be crazy to fly more missions and sane if he didn't, but if he was sane he had to fly them. If he flew them he was crazy and didn't have to; but if he didn't want to he was sane and had to. (p. 47).

Among the corollary motifs in this section is that of alleged madness. Orr is branded as crazy in the paragraph just cited. Yossarian calls Nately crazy in Chapter One; Clevinger calls Yossarian crazy in Chapter Two. Yossarian's friend McWatt is "the craziest combat man of them all probably, because he was perfectly sane and still did not mind the war." Havermeyer charges Hungry Joe with insanity, and Chief White Halfoat makes the same charge of Doc Daneeka. Indeed, by one standard or another all the characters are as mad as the world they inhabit. As in Hamlet's fictive realm, however, madness can as easily signify its opposite. At the end of this division, for instance, which coincides with the announcement of the mission to Bologna, we read the following about Yossarian:

> "He's not so crazy," Dunbar said. "He swears he's not going to fly to Bologna."
> "That's just what I mean," Dr. Stubbs answered. "That crazy bastard may be the only sane one left." (p. 114)

By and large, the characters featured in this first division are crazy in relatively harmless or even sympathetic ways. They are mostly members of Yossarian's inner circle on the Mediterranean island of Pianosa, and fall more or less into readily identifiable sub-groupings, usually pairs: Appleby and Havermeyer, both avid airmen and crack shots who love the war; Nately and Clevinger, the idealists, good but terribly naive boys who genuinely believe in the values for which they are supposedly fighting; the genuinely pathological Hungry Joe, and Dobbs, who goes "crazy in the air over Avignon"; McWatt, who loves joyriding in his B-25 and buzzing the men on the base; Huple, the fifteen-year-old pilot whose cat has a running battle with Hungry Joe; Aarfy, the soft, genial, pipe-smoking fraternity snob who completely lacks a fear of death, indeed, seems wholly insensitive to it; and Orr, a dopey, earthy, mechanically inclined gnome who seems amid his giggling to be wiser than he lets on. We meet as well a number of figures just outside Yossarian's immediate circle who, if anything, perform a larger role in the book's interwoven plots and themes: the flight surgeons Daneeka and Stubbs; the noncoms and ex-noncoms who appear to be the true administrators of military operations—the overworked Sergeant Towser and the weasley but successful punk ex-PFC Wintergreen; as well as Milo Minderbinder, who from his humble beginnings as a volunteer mess officer establishes the foundations in this section of what promises to be a major commercial enterprise. The reader also briefly becomes acquainted with Chaplain Tappman, colonels Cathcart and Korn, Generals Peckem and Dreedle and their respective entourages, all of whom will become more significant later, and a host of minor but equally Dickensian figures.

True to the already mentioned circular, redundant patterns of the rhetoric and thematic content, the plot itself progresses by epicycles within larger cycles. Chapter One, for instance, begins with Yossarian meeting the chaplain while malingering in the hospital, but Chapter Two takes the reader back to an argument Yossarian had with Clevinger before the mission to Avignon, which mission had been Yossarian's reason for seeking the hospital's sanctuary. The narrative continues to swing back and forth around the various characters, capturing bits of the past and future of each before moving on. Once the narrative has covered Yossarian's circle on Pianosa, it goes on to detail the mission over Ferrara, the first of the three central missions of the novel, and the modest foundation of Milo's syndicate, before jumping back in time to Yossarian and Clevinger in cadet school in Santa Ana, California. Here the presiding spirit is Lieutenant Scheisskopf, a softheaded monomaniac obsessed with parades, who manipulates toy soldiers and looks up arcane rules of marching while his oversexed wife sleeps with the cadets, including Yossarian. Clevinger runs afoul of Scheisskopf and finds himself the victim of an outrageous, hilarious interrogation which, in its six pages, is one of the showpieces of the novel.

Immediately thereafter comes the story of Major Major Major. The incidents that make up this pathetic farce also precede chronologically the mission to Avignon and thus Chapter One. Major Major Major received his name as a practical joke from his insufferably selfish and hypocritical father, a consummate Yankee farmer who applied his stringent values to everyone but himself. As a child and an adult, Major Major was the perfect example of an individual who did everything he was told, and was thus disliked and mistrusted by peers and authority figures alike. Having stumbled into the military, he finds himself almost immediately promoted by computer accident, then made squadron commander by Colonel Cathcart, an act which brings all the repressed hostility felt toward Major Major to the surface. He ultimately becomes a hermit, taking his meals alone, refusing to permit anyone into his office until he has slipped out a side window.

The narrative comes full circle again when the intelligence investigation into the letters Yossarian censored as Washington Irving comes to Major Major's attention. Yossarian closes the circle by tackling Major Major outside his office and asking to be grounded. All Major Major can do is offer to let Yossarian have "milk runs"; Yossarian turns him down, foreshadowing an offer near the novel's end that he will also reject.

The discussion of Catch-22, Clevinger's trial, and the sad tale of Major Major all point up another motif and theme of this book: injustice. Injustice will increasingly come to function on all levels of the story, and the many injustices perpetrated already in the first section set up the framework for the greater, even cosmic injustices to be confronted later.

This first division of the novel ends with Clevinger's disappearance, appropriately, inside a cloud, followed by a flashback to Lowery Field, Colorado, and Wintergreen. The rest of the chapter sets the stage for the second division of the novel, which is dominated by the Great Big Siege of Bologna, the second of the three missions important to the plot. The subject of death, toyed with in the first division, becomes more serious now. As the bomber group contemplates the prospect of bombing the heavily defended ammunition dumps at Bologna, the "clinging, overpowering conviction of death spread steadily with the continuing rainfall, soaking mordantly into each man's ailing countenance like the corrosive blot of some crawling disease. Everyone smelled of formaldehyde" (p. 112).

Before proceeding in earnest, the second section opens with the anecdotal chapter on Captain Black, the mean-spirited intelligence officer who is thrilled at the anguish the specter of Bologna causes in the group. Most of this chapter is taken up with his Glorious Loyalty Oath Crusade, originally initiated as a blow at Major Major, who had received the promotion to squadron commander that Black had coveted. The Glorious Loyalty Oath Crusade soon takes on a life of its own, however, satirizing in its idiotic super-patriotism the McCarthyism of the 1950s. At its peak, the Crusade forces every man to sign multiple loyalty oaths, pledge allegiance to the flag, and sing several stanzas of "The Star-Spangled Banner" to receive anything from briefings to food. The Crusade ends abruptly when the Olympian Major—de Coverley, virtually the only character who remains aloof from the injustices and oppression that reign in the book, brushes away a loyalty oath to demand food for himself and everyone else in the mess hall.

Once the Great Big Siege of Bologna gets going, it produces a series of droll and thematically demonstrative events. First, Yossarian almost succeeds in stopping the mission by nocturnally moving the bomb line on the intelligence map—another example, like the dead man in Yossarian's tent, of the artificial nature of reality as perceived by the institutions and the fictive world of the novel. This incident is followed by others reminiscent of the first division, concerning Yossarian's inner circle, and we watch Milo's syndicate grow, despite competition from Wintergreen and Milo's misguided purchase of the entire Egyptian cotton crop, which receives brief mention here but will play an important role in events later. There is also a long flashback to Ferrara and to Yossarian's accepting a medal and a promotion from Cathcart and Korn, offered to cover the embarrassment of his having flown over the target twice.

When the day of the mission to Bologna finally comes, in Chapter Fourteen, Yossarian sabotages his intercom and forces pilot Kid Sampson to turn back. The siege of Bologna is not over, however, and when Yossarian flies to the same ammunition dumps the next day he finds himself engulfed in flak. At this point occurs a scene that one critic considers the most chilling in the book. While frantically giving the pilot McWatt commands for evading the flak, Yossarian finds Aarfy once again with him in the nose of the plane, blocking the tiny crawlway that is his only route to safety. He screams at Aarfy to get out, adding, "They're trying to kill us! Don't you understand? They're trying to kill us!" But no matter what Yossarian says or how loud, Aarfy maintains he is unable to hear him. He resorts to punching Aarfy, which is "like sinking his fists into a limp sack of inflated rubber." Aarfy offers no resistance and remains, an impassive, immovable symbol of the frustration a rational mind suffers in the face of a deaf, unresponsive universe.

Following Bologna, Yossarian has his sole, droll, but ultimately sensitive encounter with Luciana, a woman he meets in Rome. No sooner does he get back to the base, than he heads for the hospital after learning that Cathcart has raised the minimum number of missions again. The novel has now circled back to the situation in Chapter One, with Yossarian malingering in the company of Dunbar, the Texan, and the soldier in white. This time, however, the setting gives rise to a number of somber, almost philosophical interludes, pursuant to the increasingly serious undertones of the narrative. First is Yossarian's meditation on death. Death is a much tidier, healthier business in the hospital: "They couldn't dominate Death inside the hospital, but they certainly made her behave." There follows a catalogue of various tragic, grisly, and mostly sudden methods of dying on the outside, including Kraft's and Mudd's exploding in mid-air, Clevinger's mysterious disappearance, and yet another teasing reference to Snowden's freezing to death "in the blazing summertime after spilling his secret to Yossarian in the back of the plane" (p. 170).

The narrative moves on, or back, to the soldier in white, who chills the men in the ward with his silence, his blankness (one is reminded of Melville's disquisition on the terror of whiteness in *Moby Dick*), and the unstated fact of the anonymity and meaninglessness of death. More is made of the nurses' practice, mentioned in the first chapter, of repeatedly interchanging the same bottles of intravenous fluid and liquid waste. The soldier in white himself represents the endless, absurd cycles of the novel.

The plight of the soldier in white leads to a discussion on the nature of cosmic justice, or the lack of it, as it turns out. Everyone in the ward agrees that he has received someone else's punishment or good fortune, leading one noncom to lament, "Just for once I'd like to see all these things sort of straightened out, with each person getting exactly what he deserves. It might give me some confidence in this universe" (p. 175). Following another catalogue of people and diseases waiting to get Yossarian is a second exchange between him and Doc Daneeka in which he begs to be grounded, only to find himself once more up against Catch-22.

The next chapter, "The Soldier Who Saw Everything Twice," also takes place in a hospital, though it leaps back in time to Yossarian's discovery of this sanctuary while yet a private at Lowery Field. Here he learns to fake a liver condition, then imitates another patient who sees everything twice, until the man dies. He finishes the chapter by taking the place of a soldier who has already died in order to give the man's family someone to visit. The chapter only moves outside the hospital once, for a Thanksgiving dialogue between Yossarian and Scheisskopf's wife in which our hero berates God for bungling the universe.

Despite the satiric edge present in these two hospital chapters, their overwhelming message is one of anger in the face of despair. Death comes in disguise in the hospital, as the soldier in white, the soldier who saw everything twice, and the dead man whose identity Yossarian takes on. It comes in many ways, as catalogued in the passages cited above. The universe and the God who created it are unjust, or at best incompetent, and death is perhaps the greatest injustice of all. Also, what were quasi-humorous devices in the first section of the novel—circularity, redundancy, doubling—have taken on a metaphorical concreteness: the bottles of fluid attached to the soldier in white, the doubling implicit in the soldier who saw everything twice. These metaphors will be developed further in the third and next part of the novel.

In section three, the narrative retreats from Yossarian to focus on a handful of characters who essentially embody the spectrum of values operating in the world of the novel: Colonel Cathcart and Lieutenant Colonel Korn, Chaplain Tappman, and Milo Minderbinder. We first meet Colonel Cathcart, who has so far functioned mainly in the background as the group commander who incessantly raises the number of missions his men have to fly. In Chapter Nineteen, named for him, we learn of the terrible insecurity that underlies his militant ambition. He lives "in an unstable, arithmetical world of black eyes and feathers in his cap, of overwhelming imaginary triumphs and catastrophic imaginary defeats" (p. 193). He wants nothing more in life than to be general, and he will do anything in his power that Lieutenant Colonel Korn tells him to do to achieve this goal.

Korn is Cathcart's "loyal, indispensable ally," an intelligent, shrewd, sardonic slob whom Cathcart utterly depends on, much to his constant distress. When he does attempt to make a move without Korn's approval, it is a short-lived plan to have the chaplain say prayers before each mission so that he, Cathcart, can get into *The Saturday Evening Post*. The dialogue between Cathcart and the chaplain demonstrates a basic conflict of the novel, particularly in this section, between the inevitable oppression of power and the weakness of the traditional ideals by which society is *supposed* to operate. The chaplain is further victimized by Korn and by his own orderly, Corporal Whitcomb; and later we will see him, like Major Major, the object of ostracism and even brutality.

One of the first items the reader learns about the chaplain is his interest in quasi-mystical phenomena. In Chapter Twenty, he briefly ponders, for the first of many times, the concepts of *deja vu*, *presque vu*, and *jamais vu*, linking them to an experience he had recently had during Snowden's funeral, where he was certain he saw a naked man in a tree. *Deja vu*, the most frequently mentioned of these phenomena, is of course the sensation of having seen something before or, to rephrase, of having seen something twice. Again the motif of recycling, of doubling, repeats itself.

Chapter Twenty-One returns to Colonel Cathcart, who is stewing over the association of Yossarian, recently named to him by the chaplain, with a couple of "black eyes," the double bombing of Ferrara and the naked man who received a medal after the mission of Avignon. This chapter contains a great deal of foreshadowing of events which have already taken place but will not be described until later in this division: the moaning in the briefing room before the mission to Avignon, the naked Yossarian's receiving a medal after the mission, and Milo's bombing of his own group.

After a brief return to Yossarian's inner circle and Dobb's plot to assassinate Cathcart, the narrative takes off on a commercial flight on which Yossarian and Orr accompany Milo. Milo is about the only character who appears to advance chronologically in the course of the novel, misleading one critic to assert that he functions on an impossible time scale that absurdly cuts across the circular chronology of the rest (Jan Solomon, "The Structure of Joseph Heller's *Catch-22*, *Critique*, 9/2 [1967], 46-57.). In fact, Milo's progress, as inexorable as the raising of the missions, puts in order the events that surround it. When seen before, in divisions one and two, he was operating an extremely efficient mess hall and founding his syndicate on pitted dates and stolen bedsheets, although hints of his future success appeared often.

Now, in Chapter Twenty-Two, entitled "Milo the Mayor," Milo's enterprise has grown into an empire, giving Heller a satirical shot at the indisputable efficacy on our planet of what he elsewhere terms "the squalid, corrupting indignities of the profit motive." Milo, it turns out, is not only the mastermind behind an incredibly widespread, ornate, and successful marketing operation, but he has as a result been made mayor of various Italian towns, Assistant Governor-General of Malta, Vice-Shah of Oran, "Caliph of Baghdad, the Imam of Damascus, and the Sheik of Araby. Milo was the corn god, the rain god and the rice god in backward regions where such crude gods were still worshipped by ignorant and superstitious people, and deep inside the jungles of Africa, he intimated with becoming modesty, large graven images of his mustached face could be found overlooking primitive stone altars red with human blood" (p. 244).

In his own way, Milo is quite moral; he refuses to do business with communists, and he disapproves of Yossarian and Orr's whoring on their commercial flight, although he contracts for the women himself in order to keep Orr out of the way. Ultimately, however, there is only one value in Milo's value system: the profit motive. Compared to the recently demonstrated inefficacy of the chaplain's religiously and ethically based code, it is obvious which actually functions in the world.

Before pursuing Milo's career further, the narrative digresses to center on the issue of values and ideals in the oft-quoted dialogue between Nately and the old man in the whorehouse. Nately, as the novel has already mentioned in passing several times, is in love with an Italian whore. He also despises the "wicked, depraved and unpatriotic old man" who lives in the brothel, and who, in a phrase reminiscent of the paradoxes of the novel's first division, "reminded Nately of his father because the two were nothing at all alike." The entire discussion between Nately and the old man is filled with such apparent contradictions. It begins with the old man's assertion that Italy will win the war because it is such a weak nation, that it will endure due to this weakness much longer than strong countries like America. As evidence, he points out that, having been defeated, Italian soldiers are no longer dying, whereas American and German soldiers are. In sharp contrast to Nately, the old man has no principles: he was a fascist when Mussolini was in power, and pro-American once the occupation began. His reply to Nately's outrage at his moral flexibility is, "I am a hundred and seven years old." His ultimate proof of the merits of his ethic is the fact of his own survival. His last words are direct inversions of Nately's:

"Anything worth living for," said Nately, "is worth dying for."
"And anything worth dying for," answered the sacrilegious old man, "is certainly worth living for." (p. 253)

Immediately thereafter, Nately reminds him of the saying, "it's better to die on one's feet than live on one's knees," to which the old man retorts, "I'm afraid you have it backward. It is better to *live* on one's feet than die on one's knees" (p. 254). The old man implies that Yossarian and Dunbar would agree, and indeed his survival ethic seems the ultimate extrapolation of their desire to stay alive at any cost.

The narrative then returns to Milo, now expanding his enterprise to include all the combat groups in the Mediterranean theater, with his own private squadron of borrowed planes. Milo has painted out the squadron emblems on the planes "illustrating such laudable ideals as Courage, Might, Justice, Truth, Liberty, Love, Honor and Patriotism . . . with a double coat of flat white and replaced them in garish purple with the stenciled name M & M ENTERPRISES, FINE FRUITS AND PRODUCE" (p. 259). No image better sums up the morally debilitating success of the ethic Milo personifies. The ideals obliterated by Milo, it merits noting, are very much those scorned by Nately's old man. The placing of "Nately's Old Man" between the two chapters featuring Milo is significant; both Milo's philosophy and the old man's are ruled by single, highly successful, and wholly pragmatic tenets—profit in the case of the former, longevity in the case of the latter.

Up to this point, Milo's enterprise has come across as amoral but basically harmless, despite intimations to the contrary. Throughout the early weeks of Milo's syndicate, in fact, Yossarian has continued to count Milo among his friends. Now, however, in Chapter Twenty-four ("Milo"), the reader learns the details of two ghastly, while laughably absurd, episodes which have so far received only brief mention. The first is the deal Milo arranges with both sides surrounding the bombing of Orvieto; Milo contracts with the Allies to do the bombing and with the German anti-aircraft forces to shoot the planes down. It is in this mission that Mudd, the dead man in Yossarian's tent, is killed (that the dead man is discussed much earlier in the novel indicates that much of Milo's story had already taken place before a number of the significant events, including the focal episodes of Bologna and Avignon).

Once more placing thematic and dramatic considerations over chronological ones, the narrative then jumps to Milo's consummate act of amorality some weeks later. Unable to unload his Egyptian cotton and facing financial ruin, Milo arranges with the Germans to bomb his own base with his own planes. In straightforward, dispassionate prose, the author describes the horror of the scene with sinister humor, adding that Milo's crews "spared the landing strip and the mess halls so that they could land safely when their work was done and enjoy a hot snack before retiring" (p. 264). Even Colonel Cathcart is outraged, and the outrage, the reader is informed in a few lines, extends back across the United States of America. Indeed, it appears that "this time Milo had gone too far," until he makes public his accounts, which reveal the tremendous profit he made from his attack. Since nothing could be more American than profit, the outrage quickly dies down.

Next comes the climactic episode of this division, which draws Cathcart, the chaplain, and Milo together around Yossarian, the occasion in which the chaplain, while presiding over Snowden's funeral, sees Milo offering choco-late-covered cotton to Yossarian, who is sitting naked in a tree, and, not knowing either Milo or Yossarian yet, misinterprets the scene as mystic revelation. We learn in detail of the chaplain's impressions of this much-foreshadowed event in the chapter entitled "The Chaplain." The chaplain stands in stark contrast to the other two characters featured in this division. Unlike aggres-sive men of action like Colonel Cathcart," who frighten him and leave him "feel-ing helpless and alone," the chaplain is weak-willed and easily cowed. "In a world in which success is the only virtue," as we have seen with Milo, the chap-lain "had resigned himself to failure." He is a spiritual man plagued by doubts, "never without misery, and never without hope." In many ways he is the most sympathetic and certainly the most sensitive, in the positive sense, character in the novel. Heller, in fact, has maintained that he thought the chaplain was the second most memorable character after Yossarian. He was surprised to find out that for most people that position belongs, ironically, to the worldly success-ful Milo.

Following more of the chaplain's lengthy speculations on *deja vu*, one learns further of his victimization at the base and of his myriad spiritual doubts. The discussion regarding values that has dominated this section is given a cosmic summation in the chaplain's observation that "[t]here were no miracles; prayers went unanswered, and misfortune tramped with equal brutality on the vir-tuous and the corrupt" (pp. 293-294). Ironically, all that sustains his faith is such bogus mystic phenomena as the naked man in the tree and a cryptic, fleeting encounter in the woods with the elusive Flume—still hiding from Chief White Halfoat—who prophesies, "I'll be back when winter comes." Indeed, the chaplain's faith seems based on his *desire* to believe; it thus differs little from the faith of other theologians of the Absurd, such as Kierkegaard and Tillich, who maintain that the only real foundation for faith is not observable fact but the will to believe itself. Faith will be an important element of the story's conclusion. With this chapter, we return to the day of the chaplain's meeting with Cathcart and thus full circle again to end the third division.

With the fourth division, the novel changes direction somewhat, and from here the progress of the narrative is more or less chronological. This section consists of two main strands: one focusing again on Yossarian's immediate circle, the other on the increasing power of General Peckem in his private war with General Dreedle, and on the rise of Peckem's new aide, the idiotic Scheiss-kopf, just transferred to the Mediterranean and now a colonel. The first chapter in this section, Twenty-six, is labeled "Aarfy" and showcases that character's insensitivity, first to Nately's romantic passion for his whore, and next, and more horrifying, to mortality. In one of the many scenes the reader confronts with the chaplain's sense of *deja vu*, Yossarian again finds himself trapped in the nose of the plane by Aarfy's immobile form. Once more Aarfy, the incom-petent navigator, has led the plane directly over an anti-aircraft emplacement. This time, however, Yossarian is wounded; the cries for assistance he directs at Aarfy receive the same deaf, blind response as in the chilling if ludicrous scene noted earlier. Even more so than before, the individual is up against a world that not only does not care about personal suffering, but does not even recognize it.

Yossarian's wound lands him in the hospital, where he and Dunbar play at changing identities by kicking noncoms out of their beds. After Yossarian and Dunbar mash Nurse Duckett, Yossarian is sent to psychoanalysis under Major Sanderson, who is of course crazier than his patient. Sanderson finally con-demns Yossarian as maladjusted, on the grounds that he is

> antagonistic to the idea of being robbed, exploited, degraded, humil-iated or deceived. Misery depresses you. Ignorance depresses you. Persecution depresses you. Violence depresses you. Slums depress you. Greed depresses you. Crime depresses you. Corrup-tion depresses you. (p. 312).

With this, Sanderson declares Yossarian insane and unfit for combat. Another man gets sent home by mistake.

The following chapter, though entitled "Dobbs," properly belongs to Orr—who, oddly, has no chapter named after him, as though he is in some sense not of this world. The chapter details at length Orr's talent for ditching damaged aircraft and the earnestness with which he makes use of the supplies on the life-boat. It catalogs Yossarian's feelings of compassion and concern for Orr, who seems like just the sort of good-natured, simple-minded fool the world is always grinding down. There follows a dialogue between the two men in which Orr once more hints that he knows more than he lets on. By the end of the chapter, Orr has disappeared in a life raft after his plane was shot down during the second mission to Avignon.

After the chapter called "Peckem," which hinges on Scheisskopf's entry into the Mediterranean, comes "Dunbar," in which a great deal happens, all of it to Yossarian's friends. There is reference to Dunbar's increasing dourness and another teasing glimpse at Snowden's death. There is the incident in which Yossarian threatens to kill McWatt during a training session; his craziness, like Dunbar's, is no longer as funny as it was earlier. Then comes McWatt's accidentally cutting Kid Sampson in half while playfully buzzing the beach, after which he purposely flies into a mountain. In this one chapter, Yossarian has lost two more comrades.

Death appears in other forms among Yossarian's inner circle as the chapters in this division march on. Doc Daneeka, listed on the log of McWatt's plane so he could receive flight pay, finds himself now officially listed as dead; Chapter Thirty-one chronicles the bureaucratic erasure of his existence. In Chapter Thirty-two, Chief White Halfoat prepares to move into the hospital to die of pneumonia, while a quartet of rambunctious new officers move into Yossarian's tent and throw out the dead man Mudd's belongings. A bit of comic and romantic relief follows in the next chapter ("Nately's Whore"), when Yossarian escapes to Rome to help Nately save his whore from a ludicrous group of naked superior officers; the whore, after a good night's sleep, wakes up finally deeply in love with Nately.

Chapter Thirty-four finds Yossarian and Dunbar malingering in the hospital again. To their surprise, the chaplain turns up as a patient, having lied his way in, and feeling very pleased with himself about this compromise with the ways of the world.

> The chaplain had sinned, and it was good. It was miraculous. It was almost no trick at all, he saw, to turn vice into virtue and slander into truth, impotence into abstinence, arrogance into humility, plunder into philanthropy, thievery into honor, blasphemy into wisdom, brutality into patriotism, and sadism into justice. (p. 372)

The relevance to the debate concerning values in the book is clear. The chaplain has bought a part of Yossarian and Dunbar's survival ethic. Still, Yossarian and Dunbar are close to the chaplain, who after all represents the most orthodox values in the novel. One suspects Yossarian of being a moralist at heart; indeed, the rapidly approaching conclusion will confirm this suspicion. Dunbar, by the way, is "disappeared" after the re-appearance of the soldier in white throws him into a violent panic.

Meanwhile, Milo cements his power with Cathcart—and thus with the side of injustice and oppression, permanently leaving Yossarian's circle of friends—by arranging to have the men fly more missions in his name to bring him some flight time and perhaps even honors. Nately takes advantage of the opportunity to volunteer for more combat, so that he can remain in the Mediterranean with his whore; as a result, he is killed when his plane is accidentally struck by one flown by Dobbs.

The injustices pile up as the chaplain is yanked away from the contemplation of Nately's demise to suffer a ridiculous interrogation, reminiscent of Clevinger's earlier in the book and with apparently the same cast of malevolent, nameless inquisitors. Having been proved guilty through a process involving no logic at all (" . . . why would we be questioning you if you weren't guilty?"), the chaplain, in a Kafkaesque non-sequitur, is told to "take a walk" while his punishment is being deliberated upon. At the chapter's end, the chaplain learns from Lieutenant Colonel Korn that Peckem has in fact replaced Dreedle as the commander of combat operations, information which sets the scene for the next chapter.

Chapter Thirty-seven, "General Scheisskopf"—at two pages the shortest in the book—ends the fourth division. In it the ultimate administrative absurdity is realized when Scheisskopf becomes head of special services, due to Peckem's move to combat, and simultaneously takes over as supreme commander, as an inadvertent result of Peckem's long-standing effort to have combat brought under special services. Even the powerful now find themselves at the mercy of the fools and low-lifes, as Peckem is viciously excoriated by Wintergreen before being ordered by Scheisskopf to make everyone march. Scheisskopf's elevation to the apex of this universe is the ultimate absurd inversion of order and logic.

With the next chapter begins the last and shortest division of the novel, that which focuses on Yossarian's final refusal to cooperate with his morally bankrupt superiors or the war effort. Yossarian's rebellion has been foreshadowed throughout the previous section in his increasingly serious obsession with staying alive, played off against the death or disappearance of virtually all his friends but Hungry Joe, who himself will suffocate under Huple's cat before the end. In fact, death—with its existentialist partner guilt—begins to accompany Yossarian almost constantly from the beginning of this division, in the physical form of Nately's whore, who holds Yossarian personally responsible for Nately's death and is trying to avenge it by killing him. Yossarian also receives, however, the unexpected reward of furtive support for his rebellion from the men in his group, even from such gung-ho types as Appleby and Havermeyer. In an inversion of value characteristic of the book, Yossarian's determined cowardice is an act of extreme courage. He has finally stood forth and said, "No!"

The novel finally touches ground, so to speak, in the next chapter, "The Eternal City," which most critics cite as the work's thematic and metaphorical climax, without question the most serious chapter of the book. It begins with Yossarian going AWOL to Rome after hearing from Captain Black that the brothel where Nately's whore had lived had been "flushed out" by M.P.s. While en route in one of Milo's planes, Yossarian suddenly understands why Nately's whore holds him responsible for Nately's death.

> Why the hell shouldn't she? It was a man's world, and she and everyone younger had every right to blame him and everyone older for every unnatural tragedy that befell them . . . . Someone had to do something sometime. Every victim was a culprit, every culprit a victim, and somebody had to stand up sometime to break the lousy chain of inherited habit that was imperiling them all. (p. 414)

Yossarian is guilty because he has not stood up earlier against the forces that killed Nately and the others; his sin is a sin of omission, of inaction.

Yossarian finds Rome in ruins and hurries to the site of the brothel, also in shambles. The only person there is the old woman who takes care of the place; she informs Yossarian that the M.P.s and *carabinieri* offered no reason or authority for their action but Catch-22—"they have a right to do anything we can't stop them from doing," the ultimate rule of injustice and oppression. What follows is a night journey through a series of vignettes pointing up the eternal misery and unfairness of human life. The images repeat themselves, appearing as though on cue: a barefoot waif trudging down the rain-soaked street, a ragged nursing mother, a group of soldiers holding down a man with convulsions, a woman pleading from a window overhead, a woman pleading with a drunken soldier on the street, a man beating a dog, a man beating a boy, a man being attacked by police, an old woman fruitlessly chasing a younger woman. Yossarian hurries away from the last scene "in shame because he had done nothing . . . . He darted furtive, guilty glances back as he fled in defeat . . . ." "Mobs with clubs were in control everywhere," he concludes.

He finally arrives at the officers' apartments only to find more injustice, and close at hand: the insensitive Aarfy has raped a helpless maid and thrown her out the window. Yossarian listens "almost with joy" as the police sirens draw near. The M.P.s break in and arrest Yossarian for being AWOL. When he ends up before Colonels Cathcart and Korn, however, he is told, in a twist reminiscent of the chaplain's interrogation, that he is to be sent home.

The next chapter, "Catch-22," begins by informing us that "[t]here was, of course, a catch," Since Yossarian has been guilty, like the Christ in Dostoevsky's "The Grand Inquisitor," of letting the other men know they have alternatives, Korn has worked out an arrangement that he himself terms "odious," by which Yossarian will be returned to the States only if he allies himself with him (Korn) and Cathcart and by extension with all the forces of hypocrisy, misplaced ambition, greed, cruelty, and injustice that rule this fictive universe. After some hesitation, Yossarian sins as the chaplain had once earlier sinned, by using "protective rationalization," albeit to a more harmful purpose. He finds a way to accept the deal. No sooner does he leave Colonel Cathcart's office than Nately's whore, symbol of Yossarian's guilt for his sins of tacit assent, stabs him.

Yossarian dimly awakes in the hospital again—put there for the second time for an actual wound—and through a fog of delirium attempts to deal with incompetent doctors, sadistic interrogators, and a mysterious, mean-faced man who repeats, "We've got your pal, buddy. We've got your pal." In a discussion with the chaplain, he realizes that "they" have gotten all his pals. He, Yossarian, is the only one left of his original circle of friends.

It is here that Yossarian finally pulls together the full story of Snowden's death, of crawling into the back of the plane while Dobbs screamed over the intercom, of treating the large wound on Snowden's thigh before noticing the wet stain under the armpit of his flak suit, and of opening the suit only to have Snowden's insides spill onto the floor of the plane. This is the much foreshadowed secret that Snowden spilled to Yossarian: "Man was matter, that was Snowden's secret. Drop him out a window and he'll fall. Set fire to him and he'll burn. Bury him and he'll rot like other kinds of garbage. The spirit gone, man is garbage. That was Snowden's secret. Ripeness was all" (p. 450). Note the use of repetition, characteristically underlining the message.

This is probably the most graphically shocking episode of the novel, and its placement near the conclusion, as well as its frequent foreshadowing throughout, gives it an importance it would not have had if buried in chronological sequence. Snowden's death, after all, took place during the first mission to Avignon, after Ferrara and Bologna but before, immediately before, we meet Yossarian in the hospital in the first chapter. Herein lies one good argument for the novel's mangled structure: on the whole, the most dramatic or serious episodes tend to cluster in the latter parts, no matter when they occurred chronologically. Though on the surface this apparently random, free-associative method does capture the chaotic spirit of the age, as Heller himself maintained in one interview ("An Impolite Interview with Joseph Heller," *The Realist*, 39 [November 1962], pp. 18-31), on a deeper level the novel has been built in more or less distinct stages, each taking thematic material from the former, recycling it, and impressing the message yet more indelibly into the reader's consciousness, like the grotesque machine in Kafka's "The Penal Colony." Thus, the narrative has unfolded from the spirited hijinks and word play of part one to the intense awareness of death of part two, the value inversions of part three, to the multiple deaths and absurdities of part four. Part five has, up through Snowden's death, finally stripped away skin and flesh, humor and rhetoric, to present the horrible heart and gut of the matter, the pitiable isolation of man in the face of his mortality.

Finally, we arrive at the last chapter, "Yossarian." This is the big scene for the heretofore minor character of Major Danby; in his dialogue with Yossarian in the hospital he reveals the difficulties of trying to compromise one's ideals in a world run by Cathcarts, Peckems, and Scheisskopfs. Yossarian reveals his own idealism at this point when he refuses to accept Korn's deal on the grounds that it would be betraying the other men. Here is where his survival ethic differs from that of Nately's old man, who chooses survival at any cost; in the end, Yossarian can only accept survival with honor. Yossarian, despite his many petty vices, proves to be a moralist at heart. Being stabbed by Nately's whore for all the sins of the world has awakened his conscience.

Danby and Yossarian go over all of the latter's rational alternatives to participation in the war; typically for this novel, the alternatives end up canceling one another out, leaving "no hope at all." Rational means having failed once more, illogic again intervenes, though this time with something positive. The chaplain bursts into the hospital room with the impossible news that Orr had reached Sweden. It is a miracle—a miracle created by Orr's decision to act in the face of hopelessness and turn Absurdity against itself. Yossarian decides to run away after all, and the chaplain to bully his superiors as they have bullied him. Yossarian, as he tells Danby, is running *to* his responsibilities, not away from them. He is turning his back not on the fight against Hitler, but on the aggrandizement of the petty fools and tyrants who are using the war for their own ignoble ends. He is rejecting against all odds the miserable ironies of human life upon which the novel has dwelt in favor of a Kierkegaardian leap of faith ("Yossarian jumped," reads the text as Nately's whore appears again), believing for belief's own sake, like the chaplain, that there is something to hope for and live for after all.

This conclusion has discomfited a number of critics, including no less a personage than Norman Mailer, who found it "hysterical, sentimental, and wall-eyed for Hollywood" ("Some Children of the Goddess," *Contemporary American Novelists*, ed. Harry T. Moore [Carbondale, 1964], pp. 13-14). Indeed, against the hopelessness of the rest of the novel, the last chapter seems out of character, too positive. Its content has been foreshadowed, however, in the chaplain's repeated faith in faith itself, as in Orr's elaborate preparations and hints in the chapter that treats his disappearance, among other things. Furthermore, Orr's escape and the hope it brings are consistent with the absurd; once more the fools have had their day. On the other hand, while the reader probably suspected all along Yossarian was a moralist at heart—one recalls his moral outrage at Milo's bombing of the group—the reader may not be prepared for his sudden "Gee whiz, I've done my part" approach to his war experience.

Other flaws have been noted in the work: stylistic excesses, errors in chronology (despite Heller's meticulous working out of the time scheme—segments of the charts he used can be seen in Kiley and McDonald's *A Catch-22 Casebook*—there are a few lapses), and the profusion and linearity of the characters. Moreover, nearly all the elements analyzed above as integral to the novel's technique,i.e. repetition, doubling, contradiction, have at one time or another been viewed as faults. Such issues will re-surface in the discussions regarding his later work.

Perhaps one of the earliest criticisms will prove the least viable: that Catch-22 so suited the era of its initial success that it cannot long survive it. That scholarly criticism of the book continues to appear in print nearly two decades later is a testament to its staying power. If nothing else, it remains a joy to read.

II: THE PLAYS

In reply to criticism that the spirit of *Catch-22* did not reflect the predominate attitude of Americans toward World War II, Heller has repeatedly noted that this novel was written during and about the fifties. In his interview with *The Realist* (cited above), he explained the difference thus:

> What distresses me very much is that the ethic that is often dictated by a wartime emergency has a certain justification when the wartime emergency *exists*, but when this thing is carried *over* into areas of peace—when the military, for example, retains its enormous influence on affairs in a peacetime situation, and where the same demands are made upon the individual in the cause of national interest . . . —when this wartime emergency ideology is transplanted to peacetime, then you have this kind of lag which leads not only to absurd situations, but to very tragic situations.

It was therefore the Cold War mentality reflected in Korea and McCarthy that Heller was criticizing and burlesquing in *Catch-22*, a mode of thought that culminated in America's involvement in Vietnam.

With his novel doing so well, Heller was able to leave the field of advertising to return to teaching. While a guest professor of literature and creative writing at Yale, he turned his pen toward the stage. Retaining his identification with the anti-war message, he created the play *We Bombed in New Haven*, first produced at Yale in 1967. In the wake of its modest success, mostly around the university theater circuit, Heller wrote a dramatic version of *Catch-22*, which was produced off-Broadway in 1971, while the Vietnam Conflict still boomed in the background. Since *Catch-22: a Dramatization* presents problems quite different from those of the novel, this study will give chronology preference and handle the plays in the order of their appearance.

In the context of 1967, the setting and characters of *We Bombed in New Haven* would have been recognizably Helleresque to anyone familiar with the author's first novel. For most of the play, the stage is an Air Force briefing room. Of the characters, the most vocal and most important are Henderson, a rebellious sergeant, and Captain Starkey, an essentially well-meaning officer who nevertheless follows orders to the letter. In the first scene we also meet the other non-commissioned airmen: Sinclair, Fisher, the smart-aleck Bailey, and the obedient, middle-aged Joe. These are joined by three or four others in uniform called the Idiots; they have no lines and do just what they are told to do. The most commanding figure onstage, literally, is the Major, who says relatively little but whose presence or absence always influences the action.

As Heller utilized prose devices—contradiction, circular reasoning, and so on—to lay the groundwork for his themes in *Catch-22*, so does he make early use of absurd stage devices that will set the viewer up, ultimately, for the thematic material to follow. The play opens, for instance, with the curtain rising halfway to reveal the actors in the process of putting the final touches on the set. After a period of embarrassed silence, Starkey turns to the Major for assistance. The Major, who then as throughout the play is forever consulting a copy of the script, orders all to finish up what they're doing so the drama can begin.

Indeed, it soon becomes apparent that the play functions simultaneously on two levels of reality. First, of course, is the fictional "reality" of the war on-stage. A second and equally insistent reality is that of the play as play, being viewed by an audience within a time frame marked by a clock on the set that keeps the actual hour. The actors shift rapidly between these realities. Shortly after the curtain finishes rising and the play proper begins, the Major informs Captain Starkey that their next mission is to bomb Constantinople. This leads to a bit of dialogue that stresses not only the reality of war, but the absurdity of war *a la Catch-22*:

STARKEY

There is no Constantinople. It's Istanbul now.
MAJOR

I know that.
STARKEY

Then why are we going there?
MAJOR

We're not going there. They are.
STARKEY

Why are *they* going there?
MAJOR

(Tapping his manuscript) Because it says so.
STARKEY

Is it dangerous?
MAJOR

Not for those who survive. For those who don't—well, I'd call that dangerous.

Here is the familiar echolalia, the quibbling over the pronouns that points up the distinction between the men who decide and the men who die, and the obvious irony of the mission being dangerous only for the non-survivors—all more or less straight out of the ethos of the earlier work. There is also a jolting hint, when the Major taps his manuscript, of the other reality operating here: the reality of the theater.

The fact of the play as play continues to erupt into the action. A few minutes into the first act, the sole female character, Ruth, a Red Cross nurse, wanders onstage as though in a trance, reciting some melodramatic but not inapt lines ("Dead . . . dead . . . dead!" and "Why can't they hear me when I speak?") while the men hoot her down. Suddenly switching to stage "realism," she complains, "If we were doing something beautiful here, I could say beautiful things like that. Instead, I've got to carry this stinking coffeepot back and forth." Shortly thereafter, following further discussion of the mission to Constantinople, Henderson insists that he's not afraid of getting killed, giving as his reason, "I'm not really a soldier . . . . I'm an *actor* . . . [ellipses Heller's] playing the part of a soldier." He then directly addresses the audience along with his fellow actors, complaining that his part is too small, pointing out his other accomplishments by asking the audience if they have seen him, according to the stage direction, in "the best-known play or movie he was actually in recently." He then argues with the other actors about their relative abilities, bolstering his side of the argument by reciting with bravado the lines, "Once more into the breach, dear friends, once more;/Or close the wall up with our English dead," from Shakespeare's *Henry V*, a far more positive and heroic war drama. This couplet will be repeated by different actors throughout the play.

Like *Catch-22*, *We Bombed in New Haven* contains numerous inversions of values and logic; in the first act, at least, as in the first section of the novel, these come across as humorous. For example:

STARKEY
Yeah! Today we're gonna bomb Constantinople right off the map.
HENDERSON
Why don't we just bomb the map?

And:

RUTH
. . . Are you married?
(Starkey gasps with surprise and spews out his coffee)
STARKEY
Jesus Christ, Ruthie! Where's your manners? That's a helluva goddam personal question to ask a gentleman you *are* sleeping with!

As in the novel, such droll exchanges create an atmosphere of irony and absurdity that will grow darker as the action proceeds.

The most frequent form of pointed humor and the one most expected in an anti-war drama is the satirization of the military mentality. Here the laughter is undercut from the beginning by the distasteful portent of the message, as for instance in the following sequence:

MAJOR
This mission to Constantinople is a military man's dream. It's a sneak attack. Are there any other questions?
BAILEY
Why are we killing Turks?
MAJOR
That's none of our business. Are there any other questions? (The men remain silent)
This is a good mission you people are flying today. If everything goes well, there shouldn't be a single thing in Constantinople left alive. This is a mission we can all be proud of.

When the first hint of tragedy appears, it too is tempered with humor and absurdity. Not long after the announcement of their mission, the men find out that Sinclair is scheduled to be killed; it's in the script. The loudest objection

Sinclair registers is that his part is thus too short; he would rather be killed in the last act.

Even within the fictive realm of the plot, the actors play different roles, occasionally even performing the parts of military men seriously. For example, during the mission to Constantinople, we see the Major relaxing over coffee and donuts. As soon as the mission ends, he begins to act out the impatient stage manager, anxious for Henderson's return on cue. When Henderson finally staggers onstage, splattered with blood, convincingly fatigued, the Major becomes the solicitous, fatherly superior officer we have seen in so many World War II movies. Henderson responds in kind.

> MAJOR
>
> Rough over Constantinople, wasn't it?
>
> HENDERSON
>
> Yes, sir. It was . . . rough.
>
> MAJOR
>
> I know. And I'm sorry. I'm proud of you today, Henderson. Very proud.
>
> HENDERSON
>
> Thank you, sir. And God bless you.

The second the Major walks offstage, however, Henderson reverts to his usual snide, swaggering self, suggesting perhaps that even in the real world of the military, the men themselves are playing roles, consciously or not.

One result of the above-discussed mingling of realities, as the play proceeds, is that the viewer is forced to accept all the realities as equally valid. These characters are airmen at war, they are actors, they are real human beings. In 1967, of course, the audience was universally aware that there *was* a war going on at that moment, several thousand miles away, and young men *were* dying. Thus, when Henderson reveals to Ruth that the blood all over him belongs to the foredoomed Sinclair, and Ruth turns to the audience to exhort, "Another young boy killed in a war. And all of you just sat there. It happened right now. Didn't you care? Doesn't it mean anything to you?"—the reality of real life and real war has been thrust into the laps of the viewers. Ruth's exhortation, the first genuinely serious moment in the play, is ironically underscored by the next lines, delivered by Starkey as he strolls onstage:

> Hey Ruthie! *Ruthie!* Take it easy, will you? What do you want from *them?* This is only a play. They never heard of this Sinclair before. He's a stranger to them. He's like a name in this newspaper.

Ruth then tests the audience's compassion with her own pathetic story: having passed her prime, being used by men who refuse to love her, looking ahead to a lonely, loveless middle and old age. She finishes this catalogue of woes with,

> So tell me, all you safe and distinguished and successful people, who sit there so amiably while I grow old and pour my heart out, and while a nice young man who never did you any harm is ordered to fly to Constantinople and be killed—what do I do now?

She is begging the audience to commit themselves to involvement. Ironically, just as an important aspect of the play's message is being pressed home, the tone abruptly changes; Ruth informs Starkey that they are having a baby, he proposes in a scene of arch-sentimentality, they embrace "in trite, theatrical tradition," and stroll offstage arm-in-arm singing "My Blue Heaven" under the Major's approving supervision. The role-playing of the theater—in this case, in its most romantic form—displaces the more negative and believable reality of Ruth's pained speeches.

It is at this point that the audience is introduced to a pair of characters who step in from the "real world," but who will gradually slip into convincing roles in the war drama. These are the Sportsmen, the Hunter and the Golfer, two middle-aged, middle-class types dressed and armed per their respective hobbies, apparently financial backers of the play. They seem initially sheepish and out-of-place on-stage, though obviously tickled to be there. Emphasizing the dual reality in operation here, their first dialogue with the Major is full of puns on military and theatrical terminology. For instance, discussing the success of the play, the Golfer asks, "Suppose we bomb here?" to which the Major replies, "I'll blast them off the map," appending, "We just killed them in Constantinople, didn't we? I can kill these people as well." The Golfer and the Hunter then express an interest in having more of "a part in this," since they have "never really been in one before." The Major agrees and puts them through a few drilling maneuvers. The ambiguity of "this" and "one" in their requests is purposeful: they could be speaking either of the play or the war.

The line separating these two realities grows thinner when Henderson reappears somewhat later than the rest of the men, dazed and distressed because he cannot find backstage the actor who played Sinclair. Starkey comes on explaining that Sinclair was never real since he, like all of them, was an actor. The realities mingle further in the exchange that follows, as Starkey continues to try to convince Henderson, in contradictory terms, of Sinclair's unreality:

STARKEY

There *was* no Sinclair. He never lived. He didn't die.

HENDERSON

Then who did we just bury?

STARKEY

Sinclair. But he wasn't real. It didn't happen.

HENDERSON

Why did we bury him?

STARKEY

Because he was killed.

And so forth.

The equation of war and play persists when Starkey passes out athletic equipment to the men, "to put you all in just the right frame of mind for the big mission to Minnesota." As always, the Idiots are the first to take the equipment seriously, and they begin playing basketball. Gradually the name characters get involved, until, when a football comes into play, even Henderson joins in. Then Starkey tosses out infantile items: building blocks, rattles, plastic harmonicas, and pacifiers. This time Henderson remains aloof as the others regress.

Having presumably gotten everyone into the "right frame of mind," Starkey then introduces the "grown-up" game of "Time Bomb." First a large black ball is tossed out which the men throw to one another until a bell rings. Then another black ball is thrown around until a bell rings again. This time, however, Captain Starkey frantically orders the man holding the ball to throw it into the wings, where an explosion sends smoke billowing onto the stage. A third ball enters the circle of men, but this time no one knows whether it is a bomb or not. There is a moment's tension after the bell goes off, before Starkey yells and tosses the ball into the audience. He explains once again, chuckling, that this is only a play and no one really gets hurt. With this reminder, the first act ends.

This lengthy, somewhat too insistent analogy between war and infantile play continues into the beginning of the second act: following the rolling of a pair of bowling balls across the stage, the men gradually appear, still playing with the toys and athletic equipment. Fisher comes on with his younger brother, named Young Fisher, who early quotes a line from Shakespeare of questionable aptness ("Those are pearls that were his eyes") to prove his ability as an actor, i.e., soldier. Henderson returns, having found as yet nothing of Sinclair but his street clothes. The Sportsmen reappear as well, now dressed from the waist up like M.P.s, and march in cadence around the stage, pleased and embarrassed when the men form a mocking parade behind them. After the Major turns up, munching on a pacifier, Henderson notes aloud for the first time how young Young Fisher is, around thirteen. Young Fisher replies, in a line worthy of *Catch-22*, "They said it would disrupt my life less if I got killed sooner." Shortly thereafter, Henderson wonders whether the men's participation in the war/play makes any of them any smarter than the Idiots.

The drama finally returns to major key with the announcement by the old-timer Joe that Henderson is due to die in the next mission. It is revealed a few lines later that Joe will also be killed, as will one of the Idiots. Henderson refuses to fly the mission, insisting, "This is a stupid part in a stupid show, and I'm not going ahead with it!" Joe and one of the Idiots applaud, reminding one perhaps of the support Yossarian received during his rebellion. Also reminiscent of the novel is Henderson's assertion that Starkey's job was better than his, since his was to get killed while Starkey ate coffee and donuts and got the girl (as it was Wintergreen's and Milo's duty to make a profit, the other men's to get blown up in combat). Foreshadowing the end of the play, Starkey attempts to act fatherly to Henderson, to which attempt Henderson responds, "I've already had a father. I don't trust *you* either." Starkey then draws a long analogy between drama and life by telling an apocryphal story about Augustus Caesar on his deathbed. To Henderson's pleas for more time, Starkey replies with stale aphorisms and remarks like, "The play's the thing, and the play must go on." Starkey is brought up short by the child-like Young Fisher's pointed question, "Are you going to kill me, too?" "Me?" Starkey answers. "No, of course not. I don't kill anybody. We won't kill you until we have to."

The plot, so to speak, thickens when Henderson disappears during a change of scenery. The Major calls on the Sportsmen, now fully dressed as M.P.s and with a sudden, chilling air of competence, sends them in pursuit. Fisher and Young Fisher volunteer to die in Henderson's place, leading to a silly argument in which both Bailey and Joe complain that Young Fisher is too fresh and inexperienced to merit being killed next. The Major has the curtain closed while Henderson is being sought, and pulls Starkey downstage to rage about the importance of Henderson being killed on cue. Starkey is stunned, confused: "Are you acting now? Or do you really mean everything you're saying?" The Major turns the argument against Starkey, telling him he only needs to follow orders without question and adding,

> You're conditioned to agree and you're trained to do as you're told.
> You like the pay and the prestige, and you do enjoy your job here,
> remember? So you'll stay right where you are, do just what you're
> supposed to, and continue reciting your lines exactly on cue—just
> as you're doing right now.

Starkey protests, but the Major shows him that even his protests are in the
manuscript.

After the Major departs, Starkey has his first serious moment with the audience, with a monologue in blank verse reminiscent of T.S. Eliot that ends,

> I'm not sure I like it here any more,
> Squeezed in between the curtain
> And the edge of the stage,
> Squeezed into this small narrow role,
> Pressed into a tight uniform,
> Between the curtain
> And the edge of the stage,
> And forced to say,
> "Yes, sir."

Starkey, it should be recognized by this time, is comparing the narrowness of
his options as an actor on-stage with the narrowness of his role as a military
man. From this point on, Starkey, up to now a marginally unsympathetic
character, starts becoming the focus of the audience's involvement. At the same
time, humor, already scarce in the second act, completely disappears.

The curtain rises again to reveal Ruth in her dressing room, where Starkey
joins her. She is on the verge of hysteria because of the repeated sinister knocks
and voices at her door—the Sportsmen, searching for Henderson. Ruth finally
confesses to Starkey that Henderson, at the play's beginning also her lover,
is indeed hiding in her closet. When he appears, in civilian clothes which,
he maintains ironically, "used to be very popular," he announces he's quitting
the play/war:

> I don't want to make believe any more. I'm tired of playing sol-
> dier—like those two jokers out there. I don't want to make believe
> I'm to be killed. I don't want to make believe I'm *not* going to be
> killed. I don't want to make believe I'm killing other people, and then
> have to make believe I'm not killing them.

A careful perusal of these lines shows that Henderson is speaking more of
the war than the drama now. To Ruth's request that Starkey help Henderson
escape, Starkey underscores his sins of omission/compliance by shouting,
"Goddammit—I'm not the villain around here! I'm not the one whose running
things! Am I? *Am I*! I just do what I'm told to do, along with everyone else."

Starkey does promise to help Henderson, however, provided Henderson will
allow himself to be escorted by the Sportsmen to the Major. Henderson reluctantly agrees, and the scene shifts back to the briefing room. Here Starkey ends
up backing down before the Major's greater authority. Suddenly, the Sports-

men turn ugly, having learned their roles well indeed, and execute Henderson by shotgun. Bleeding profusely all over Starkey, Henderson writhes through a long death agony. Pointing to the finally still corpse, the Major orders, "Get that junk out of here," a line he had used earlier to clear stage props. The men applaud Henderson for his acting, then are stunned to discover he is really dead. Henderson is dragged offstage following the Major's command that they "lug the guts" off, an allusion to *Hamlet* that seems inappropriate and gratuitous here.

With Henderson unexpectedly gone, Starkey now becomes the play's main character, and we enter the drama's final, quintessential, and most serious scene. Henderson's replacement is sent on-stage and turns out to be Starkey's own son by Ruth, born earlier in the play but already nineteen years old. Starkey is forced to tell the boy that he is scheduled to be blown up in a plane. When the son protests, Starkey insists, "It's not my fault." The dialogue proceeds:

> STARKEY'S SON
> What were you doing when all this was happening?
> STARKEY
> My job, I guess.
> STARKEY'S SON
> Pop, you had nineteen years to save me from this. Why didn't you do something?
> STARKEY
> It didn't seem possible.

Starkey finds himself in the position of *Catch-22*'s Major Danby, committing the sin of doing nothing to oppose injustice, war, etc., the sin of compliance that Yossarian attempted to fight by running away. True to the spirit of 1967, the argument here is also a generational one. At one point, Starkey replies to his son's vehement accusations with "Shut up! You're my son!" to which the son retorts, "*You* shut up! You're my father!" One recalls Henderson's earlier implication to Starkey that he would not trust the captain while the latter was acting fatherly because he could not trust his own father. Such lines reflect the widely held contention, tied to the anti-war sentiments of the period, that sons were paying with their lives for the sins of their fathers.

As with Henderson, Starkey does finally agree to help his son escape. Twice, however, his son is brought back by the Sportsmen as the replacement, each time under a different name. When Starkey asks, for the record, "What's your name, son?" the boy bitterly answers, "Son." He is, in fact, everyone's son. Again, as with Henderson, Starkey backs down before the Major's authority, and finally tells his son, "You have to go." "Then will you get angry now?" the son demands. "Will you at least raise your voice? Won't you do anything to save me? Won't you do something to show you even care?" Starkey asks for suggestions, then refuses his son's request that he smash the Major's face in. Starkey insists that his son's fate is determined by the script and is thus not his fault. Having done his best to wash his hands of responsibility, Starkey allows the Major to lead off his still angry son. Immediately one hears the roar of jet planes, indicating a contemporary war. Starkey turns to the audience for his last speech, in which he further attempts to absolve himself by observing,

Now, none of this, of course, is really happening. It's a show, a play in a theater, and I'm not really a captain. I'm an actor . . . . Do you think that I, _____ _____ (Repeats his real name) would actually let my son go off to a war and be killed . . . and just stand here talking to you and do nothing? . . . Of course not! There is no war taking place here ri—

He breaks off at the sound of "a single, great explosion" in the distance, which represents not only the death of Starkey's son but the deaths of all the sons then across the ocean in Vietnam. The bitterness and resignation in Starkey's last remarks demonstrate that he has been unable to convince even himself; after noting that no one in the play has really been killed, he adds, sardonically, "Nobody has ever been killed." A few lines further on, he picks up his portfolio and newspaper, walking offstage like any man heading home after a day's work. With that, the drama ends.

The play has several fine touches, particularly the confusion of theater and reality early in the first act and the attendant humor. Not so successful is the sequence involving the athletic equipment and toys which, although it extends the metaphor of war as "playing," makes its point too quickly and then goes on too long. Also ineffective and of dubious artistic purpose is the frequent use of rarely apt literary allusions, mostly to Shakespeare (*Hamlet, Henry V, The Tempest*) and T. S. Eliot (*The Waste Land*). One suspects Heller of sacrificing the esthetic whole for the sake of certain limited effects.

Some might also find troublesome the relatively sudden shift of focus, in the next to last scene, from Henderson to Starkey. It can be argued, however, that Starkey and Henderson have taken turns dominating the stage to some extent—they are both lovers of Ruth in the first act—although Henderson has been a more sympathetic character throughout. This fact, of course, makes his center-stage murder in the second act that much more effective dramatically. It also allows Starkey to command the audience's attention for the moral battle with his conscience which stands at the climax here, as did a similar conflict in *Catch-22*. In Starkey's case, however, he gives in to the oppressive rule of authority; that is, he loses the battle.

What hurts the play most, ultimately, is the passage of time, ironically one of its secondary themes. The reality of an ongoing and, in particular, an un-popular war is what gives this play much of its dramatic and emotional clout. With the Vietnam experience by and large no more than an unpleasant memory today, the play has lost much if not most of what made it effective—and affec-tive—at the time it was first performed. It is not just an anti-war play, but an anti-Vietnam War play; in that sense it lacks the greater universality of *Catch-22* and is less likely to survive.

With *Catch-22: a Dramatization*, first performed in East Hampton, New York, on July 13, 1971, Heller produced his third work on the anti-war theme. At the time of this play's appearance, the novel had been in circulation for a decade, and the film version directed by Mike Nichols was still, if not in first run, at least turning up regularly in the second-string movie houses. Confronting the challenge of creating something new out of already heavily worked and very familiar materials, Heller stresses in his preface to the play the themes of in-justice and the abuse of authority, specifically the "unchecked misuses of authority in an atmosphere of war." Heller discusses at great length such exem-plary cases as Lt. Calley and Vietnam, Muhammed Ali's losing his title for resisting the draft, and the trials of Angela Davis, the Berrigan brothers,

Dr. Spock, the Chicago Seven, Bobby Seale, and Daniel Ellsberg. He makes the sardonic comment that "in this free enterprise culture of ours, reputable citizens are not supposed to pay for their principles; they are supposed to profit from them. Otherwise, what good are they?" (New York: Delacorte, 1973, p. xviii.) This play too, then, is firmly rooted in the experience of the late Sixties.

Obviously, the novel *Catch-22* presents a number of difficulties which do not permit simple transplantation to the stage: its size, its twisted chronology, the number of characters, its rapid and wide-ranging changes of scene, and so on. Heller mentions some of the decisions he had to make, the results of which are clear in the course of the play. First of all, the dramatization has only 40 characters, all played by ten men and two women. Second, events take place in apparent chronological sequence, meaning that often they do not occur in the same sequence as in the novel. In the play, for instance, Clevinger dies during Bologna, and it is he that is being buried when Milo approaches Yossarian about his chocolate-covered cotton. Furthermore, there is no foreshadowing of events, so much a part of the novel; in fact, so telescoped is the action tht we often no sooner meet a character than he is killed. This happens even with such central figures as Clevinger, Nately, and McWatt. Indeed, a number of characters turn up only once or in strictly limited guises. Aarfy, for instance, appears for the first time near the play's end, and then only to rape and kill the maid off-stage. Gus and Wes, Daneeka's assistants, show up only to tell Daneeka he was killed in McWatt's plane, here blown up over Avignon. Captain Black appears only to pass on Cathcart's missions, his most frequent line being, "Eat your livers, you bastards! Ha, ha, ha!"

There is a great deal of condensing, of grafting characteristics of several characters from the novel onto one in the play. Yossarian, for example, has Hungry Joe's screaming nightmares. The Texan is also one of the C.I.D. (intelligence) men in the hospital as well as one of the sinister, oppressive figures that appear in Yossarian's delirium after he is stabbed by Nately's whore. Doc Daneeka moves to the woods after his "death" to live like the Captain Flume of the novel, and even has Flume's lines ("Chaplain: What do you do when it rains./Doc Daneeka: I get wet."). Major Major is not only the elusive hermit, but takes Major Danby's place as apologist in the story's last scene, where Yossarian decides to desert. Nurse Duckett stands in for Scheisskopf's wife while Yossarian berates the stupidity and cruelty of God.

The play makes visual some material that is more narrative in the novel. At the beginning of Act Two, for instance, Yossarian introduces Nately with the familiar line, "He had a bad start—he came from a good family," after which Nately listens to his parents, who are on-stage, repeat the admonitions about associating only with the best people that one finds reference to in the novel. The necessity of making narrative visual also leads Heller to use the chaplain and Wintergreen for purposes of exposition; most of the time the chaplain appears on-stage, it is to read aloud a letter he is in the process of writing to his wife, reporting such matters as the raising of missions, Clevinger's death, and one of Yossarian's flights to the hospital. In the play version Wintergreen is more clearly in charge of the administration of the war, and occasionally stands at center stage to pass correspondence back and forth, most notably in the exchange of letters that follows Doc Daneeka's reputed death.

Now and then Heller goes too far and makes concrete a metaphor that was more successful as mere language. Perhaps the worst example of this is Colonel

Cathcart's first entrance, "wearing a black circle around one eye and an Indian headdress with several feathers." Later in his office, there is some juggling of feathers and "black eyes." This metaphor for Cathcart's obsession with his self-image loses its significance altogether when Milo, inspired by Cathcart's headdress, wanders off-stage in a trance to capture the feather market. The play contains a few more of these facile and unfortunate jokes. Aarfy, for instance, during his brief appearance in the last act, does little but bark, "Arf! Arf! Arf!" This may be a reference to his beast-like insensitivity, dealt with at some length in the novel, but here it just seems a suspiciously insistent pun on his already punning name.

The scenes that work the best are those lifted as dramatic units from the novel: Yossarian's teasing dialogue with Luciana, his psychiatric session with the neurotic Major Sanderson, his taking the role of the dying Italian soldier for the family visit, and the chaplain's interrogation, to name the most memorable. The last is in fact the actual climax of the play's stated theme, the misuse of authority, here underlined by the chaplain's paraphrase, in a letter to his wife, of the first line of Kafka's *The Trial* ("Someone must have been telling lies about me, for without having done anything wrong . . .") In an effort, perhaps, to catch the ever-flowing, free-associative spirit of the novel, Heller has reduced the rest of the plot to a string of walk-ons. Few characters appear more than once, only the likes of the chaplain, Cathcart and Korn, Milo, Major Major, Nurse Duckett, and, of course, Yossarian. Necessarily, most of the novel's characters do not appear at all. Still, a few seem conspicuous in their absence— Dunbar and Orr, for instance, and any one of the generals—Peckem, Dreedle, or Scheisskopf—would have been welcome. In Heller's defense it must be noted that he was forced to cut the script down repeatedly to fit into the time allowed by the stage, a feat which undoubtedly required many difficult and reluctant excisions and revisions, as his introducton suggests.

It must also be mentioned that the play does succeed in keeping the viewer off-balance, whirled about in somewhat the same way as is the reader of the novel. Again, the necessities of theatrical form prevent the exploitation of a number of the original work's thematic and rhetorical devices; almost all that survives of the doubling and *deja vu* so central to the book is the chaplain's periodic mention to his wife, that he is seeing or imagining the same things twice, the soldier who sees everything twice, and the utilization of one actor to play all the men who die (Clevinger, Nately, McWatt, the soldier who sees everything twice, and Snowden). And while the smaller scope of the stage prevents the portrayal of many of the broadest, most memorable episodes—Milo's bombing of the group, Yossarian's walk through The Eternal City, and so on— the play does contain much the same proportions of humor and despair.

It is difficult to imagine anyone approaching this play without an awareness of the novel, and in any comparison of the two the dramatization is bound to come out wanting on nearly all counts. Even bearing in mind the large differences in requirement between the genres of fiction and drama, *Catch-22: a Dramatization* is simply not as great a work of theater as *Catch-22*, the novel, is a work of prose. The play may have much of the novel's energy, but it lacks the other's depth and scope, not to mention technique.

Despite certain general similarities in theme and presentation, *Catch-22: a Dramatization* is qualitatively different from *We Bombed in New Haven*, and in a number of ways more polished and less polemical. While the earlier play may be a more pointed commentary on its decade, and may therefore have played more dramatically before contemporary audiences, it may require another period of unpopular war to work so well again. *Catch-22: a Dramatization* shares with its parent work a somewhat greater universality, albeit limited to the issue of individual responsibility in the face of injustice. It operates, however, on a much less affective level than either the novel or the other play.

Catch-22, the novel, so dominates Heller's work of the Sixties that it is doubtful the plays will ever be regarded as anything but appendices to that work, interesting primarily as artifacts of Heller's perception of his audience and his audience's perception of the major issues of the time, and secondarily as the products of a sideline to the author's main course of development.

III:
SOMETHING HAPPENED

Something happened to the United States of America between 1971, the year of *Catch-22: a Dramatization*, and 1974, which marked the publication of Heller's second novel. The country had finally wound down its participation in the unpopular conflict in Vietnam, a retreat that for most signaled the country's first defeat in war. The voters of the nation had overwhelmingly returned Richard Nixon to the White House, only to watch for the next two years the unfolding of Watergate, perhaps the largest (at least the most complicated) scandal in the history of the presidency. Americans had been reminded in a small way of the indelicate balance of the prosperity they had enjoyed since World War II, as they suffered in the dark winter of 1973-1974 the Arab oil embargo, shortages in a number of goods from meat to (it was rumored) toilet paper, and a mounting spiral of inflation and economic stagnation still with us at the end of the decade. Even the New Left, so full of hopes and answers at the beginning of the Seventies, had splintered and disappeared from the front page—with the unfortunate exception of the Symbionese Liberation Army—by the time of Nixon's resignation.

The nation was in the doldrums in 1974, with neither the anger nor the ebullience of the previous decade. Its mood was self-absorbed, self-pitying, and self-abusive.

Joseph Heller's second novel, *Something Happened*, fit the tenor of 1974 as well as *Catch-22* did that of, say, 1964. Like the first novel, however, it too had been begun several years before publication. Mention of it is made as early as 1962, in a *Newsweek* review of *Catch-22*. At that time, Heller apparently wanted to capture in prose the circa-1960 middle-class business- and family-man, as he had earlier delineated the Cold War ethic of the Fifties. With the tremendous artistic and financial success of *Catch-22* and his continued identification with the anti-war message in the plays, Heller saw no need, artistically or financially, to ready the novel for publication until the early Seventies, after he had settled into a teaching position at the City College of New York.

Like the time in which it appeared, *Something Happened* lacks both anger and ebullience. Whatever the novel is, it is *not* another *Catch-22*, and many readers coming to it with that expectation have been disappointed. The book is structured as a long monologue told by one Bob Slocum, a detestable while ultimately pathetic WASP with all the trappings of "the Good Life," who spends 530 pages (in the 1975 Ballantine edition) telling the reader about his fears, his memories, his disappointments, his promiscuous and mostly adulterous sexual encounters, and his struggles at the office with his colleagues and superiors and at home with his wife and children. One of the ironies of the title is that, up to the novel's quick, surprising climax, very little actually does happen. *Something Happened* presents a bleak landscape of one man's psyche, for all its internal movement fairly static. Heller summed up the difference between this novel and his first one in a brief interview with George Plimpton in *The New York Times Book Review* (6 Oct. 1974, pp. 2-3, 30); he noted that while *Catch-22* "is concerned with physical survival against exterior forces or institutions which want to destroy life or moral self," *Something Happened* is "concerned very much with interior, psychological survival" on a far more personal battlefield.

The initial critical response to this novel more or less established the parameters of the issues and problems it presents. On one hand were the large number who found the monotony and redundancy of the narrative deadening. The unkindest cut of all in this direction came from Nelson Algren, one of the earliest defenders of *Catch-22*, who wrote, "Slocum's complaints and Slocum's hopes, unlike Yossarian's complaints and hopes, possess no life . . . . [A]ll are offered with a repetitiousness that brings the reader close to asphyxiation" (*Critic*, 33 [Dec. 1974], 90-91). Another reviewer suggested that it was impossible to write a good novel about someone who is standing still. Yet another, Gene Lyons, thought the novel offered "a parade of stock characters" who "were one-dimensional to the point of bathos," and while it did demonstrate Heller's "best effects: his fondness for paradox and his characters' habit of self-revelation by self-contradiction . . . after a while it gets predictable, then very old" (*The Nation*, 16 June 1979, p. 727).

Others, while conceding the work was repetitious, also found it well-written, perceptive, affecting, and remorseless. Among those who viewed the monotonous nature of the narrative in a genuinely positive light was Kurt Vonnegut, who observed that Slocum embodies the sterility, the "unrelieved misery," of middle-class life in the postwar period. For Vonnegut, *Catch-22* and *Something Happened* embrace a two-volume history of their—his and Heller's—generation, from the dangers, horrors, and thrills of World War II to the gray flannel purgatory of the stable, prosperous, dully hypocritical world that followed. At the most enthusiastic end of the spectrum stood reviews such as John W. Aldridge's in *Saturday Review/World* (19 Oct. 1974, pp. 18-21). He called *Something Happened* "the most important novel to appear in this country in at least a decade," viewing the whole as "Dostoevskian in its compulsiveness and pathological morbidity." Whether one views the novel as Dostoevskian or merely suffocating, however, it does possess, upon close reading, a complexity that its superficial uniformity of tone tends to conceal.

The story begins with a brief introductory section entitled "I get the willies." Here we first learn from the narrator that he "gets the willies" from closed doors; he is convinced that behind them are brewing disasters that will have horrible consequences for him. In the anecdotes that follow he attempts to uncover the root cause of this fear, but only finds a series of primal scenes in which he discovered, on the other side of closed doors, his father (who died shortly thereafter) in bed with his mother, his older sister naked after a bath, and his brother furtively engaged in sex with a younger girl in a coal shed. The subject of closed doors leads him to a short disquisition on a theme that he will return to often: his fear of finding out things he'd rather not know, particularly in the case of children who might turn out to be his. "Something did happen to me somewhere," he says, "that robbed me of confidence and courage and left me with a fear of discovery and change and a positive dread of everything unknown that may occur. I dislike anything unexpected" (p. 6; all page references are to the Ballantine edition [New York, 1975]).

His dread of uncovering the worst is summed up at the end of the introduction with a story in which he was forced to set traps for mice whose existence was never proven. He hated the dubious necessity of setting the traps; he hated the possibility of finding a dead mouse in one some morning. But what he feared most of all was that one day he would find a live mouse near a trap and "have to do something about it." Already, in the few pages of this first section, the fear of the unknown and the unpleasant, which includes the fear of change, has been linked to sex, guilt, mortality, and the dread of having to act, which in turn assumes a reluctance to take responsibility for his actions. These interconnected motifs set up the framework for the novel's themes, and the motifs themselves will recur over and over in the course of the narrative.

Heller has stated on more than one occasion that he usually conceives the first line of a novel first, after which the rest falls into place. Originally, *Something Happened* began in Heller's mind with the sentences that open the next section, "The office in which I work":

> In the office in which I work there are five people of whom I am afraid. Each of these five people is afraid of four people (excluding overlaps), for a total of twenty, and each of these twenty people is afraid of six people, making a total of one hundred and twenty people who are feared by at least one person. Each of these one hundred and twenty people is afraid of the other one hundred and nineteen, and all of these one hundred and forty-five people are afraid of the twelve men at the top who helped found and build the company and now own and direct it. (p. 9)

These widespread fears are rooted in everyone's insecurity; everyone has "the whammy" on everyone else, and everyone except those at the very top apparently has the same fears about being "found out" and kicked out of the company's cosmos. As Slocum phrases it, "I have a feeling that someone nearby is soon going to find out something about me that will mean the end, although I can't imagine what that something is" (p. 11). Ironically, the one person in Slocum's office who is least terrified and happiest at her work is a secretary, Martha, who is slowly going crazy. No one wants to take the responsibility to fire her or otherwise ease her out of the company. Slocum shares with his colleagues the horror that someday someone, and perhaps even he, will have to take some action regarding her.

Slocum appears to have with all others in this environment a love-hate relationship based on mutual dependency and mistrust, and in his company such relationships are evidently the rule. The most important figure to him, the one most potentially dangerous, is Jack Green, who heads the department that contains Slocum's division. Green "is notorious for being frank and unkind . . . . He would rather make a bad impression than no impression." He annually, publicly asserts his power over Slocum by refusing to let him speak at the company convention, a recurring act which Slocum finds detestable and unforgivable. Green rarely confronts Slocum at any point in the novel without insulting and bullying him. According to Slocum, Green wants everybody "adoring and scared stiff," though like a good would-be Machiavellian, he would rather be feared than loved. Green is burdened by fears of his own, however. More than anything, he wants to be vice-president, and he is forever fawning on his superiors, such as the ever-present, nobly-named Arthur Baron. As Slocum tells us:

> He knows he does this and is ashamed and remorseful afterward
> for having demeaned himself in vain; he is willing to demean him-
> self, but not in vain. Often, he will turn perverse afterward and
> deliberately offend somebody important in order to restore what
> dignity and self-respect he feels he has lost as a man. He is a baby.
> (p. 34)

And yet for all this he is also the man that Slocum respects and likes the best, which does not stop Slocum, nevertheless, from trying to get the whammy on Green by playing off his insecurities.

One of the people Slocum uses in the effort is another close associate, the head of the Sales Department, Andy Kagle. Green considers Kagle his compe-titor, and is convinced furthermore that Kagle has the ear of top management; for one thing, Kagle is a church-going Protestant in a Protestant company, while Green is the sole Jew. But, as Slocum himself is only too aware, Kagle is too lax and gauche to impress any of the higher-ups. Kagle is prone to wearing out-of-style, poorly fitting, unmatched clothing. He has a congenital malfor-mation of the hip that causes him to limp. He is bigoted, awkward around people, and given to bad jokes. He performs his work adequately, but takes off frequently on phony business trips which he spends whoring. He is also too nice to get rid of the alcoholic, Red Parker, and the old man, Ed Phelps, in his department.

Slocum's relationship with Kagle is exactly the opposite of Slocum's with Green. Slocum and Kagle are comfortable and trusting with each other. Kagle does not scare Slocum, and for this reason—as well as the pitiful appearance Kagle makes—Slocum neither respects Kagle nor particularly likes him. In fact, Slocum forever suppresses the sadistic desire to kick Kagle in his crippled leg.

Surrounding Slocum, Green, and Kagle are a number of other office charac-ters, ranging from Arthur Baron at the top to Phelps, Parker, and the other salesmen at the bottom. The important ones have, like Green, the names of colors: Johnny Brown, the broad-shouldered, tough-talking, mid-range execu-tive who frightens everyone and who is related to the powerful background figure, Lester Black; and Horace White, who derives most of his clout and secu-rity from owning a substantial share of the company.

It is a good company, Slocum tells us, as he lists the number of breakdowns, suicides, divorces, and deaths from both accidental and medical causes that take place among its employees every year. It is a benevolent company, hiding ineffective older executives behind nonexistent functions rather than firing them, letting younger personnel who are not working out seek better jobs else-where, and looking the other way before the multifarious sins of its people provided they remain discreet. Still, nearly everyone employed there is un-happy. Slocum, even though he has no further ambitions and thus minimizes his disappointments, would rather die right away than spend a lifetime there. He has no plans to leave, however: "I have the feeling now that there is no place left for me to go."

Near the end of this section, Slocum is called to Arthur Baron's office. En route he is stopped by Kagle, Green, and Brown, the first two worried about Baron, the last about Kagle. Baron tells Slocum he is being groomed to replace

Kagle. Slocum, of course, lies to Kagle, Green, and Brown about the portent of the meeting, though he does, in what seems a display of generosity, beg Kagle to shape up. Back in his own office, Slocum briefly reviews his personal problems and the decline of American society. But what's most important to him, and what looms foremost in his thoughts as the section ends, is that he wants the job he has been offered. It is an end in itself and for the moment all that really matters.

In the next few sections, which together make up the largest part of the novel, Slocum talks about his family members, ostensibly one by one but with the inevitable mingling. While doing so, he continues to reveal as much if not more of himself. In "My wife is unhappy," after a brief introductory summary of her aging, drinking, and incompetent flirtation, a remark of hers leads him to a discussion of a quirk of his with important thematic applications. It happens that Slocum tends to adopt the characteristics, particularly the negative ones, of other people; he takes on accents, gestures, personality traits, even stammers and Kagle's limp, but only until someone with stronger characteristics comes along. In a free-associative jump, Slocum compares this idiosyncrasy of his with his teenage daughter's desire to blend into the environment of her peers. Slocum fears he may in fact have no character of his own: "I often wonder what my own true nature is," he muses, "Do I have one?" and "The problem is that I don't know who or what I really am."

Slocum declares that he still finds his wife attractive, though he doubts he loves her. In fact, he uses the section nominally devoted to her to discuss at length his marital infidelities and his past desires. Of the latter, the most vivid and recurrent concerns his first real sexual passion, with a twenty-one-year-old co-worker named Virginia ("Virgin for short, but not for long," she would quip) when he was a tender, naive seventeen-year-old employed in the records office of an insurance company. Virginia was the consummate tease; she knew exactly what to say or do to keep the young Slocum in a perpetual state of excitation, from rubbing her knees against him to telling him stories of her past sexual exploits. Periodically, frequently, Slocum would meet her on the staircase outside the office for some heavy petting, which would last for no more than a few seconds before Virginia grew frightened and raced back to her desk, only to begin the cycle again with winks and suggestive remarks. She told him repeatedly that she would have sex with him only if he got a hotel room; he always replied he did not know how. He never did have sex with Virginia, in fact. He left the office to participate in World War II, and when he returned she had committed suicide.

Slocum's memory wanders often to Virginia in the course of the narrative. He keeps wondering what it would have been like to make love to her; he cherishes in retrospect her ability to keep him excited, and daydreams about her regularly at home and in the office. He even maintains he is in love with her. On the other hand, he observes that if she were still alive, "she would be stout and wrinkled and suffer from constipation, gallstones, menopause disturbances, and bunioned feet, and I more than likely would not wish to see her." He adds: "Everything passes. (That's what makes it endurable.)" He concludes ultimately, in a later passage, that he is "glad she is dead, because otherwise I might not be [in love with her], and then I would have no one."

Slocum's present sex life is very active—and empty. In the first encounter mentioned in the book, Slocum accompanies Kagle to a pair of Cuban whores. Slocum does not find whores much fun and always leaves as soon as he's finished, but he goes to them when he has the chance. In an episode described near the end of the novel, he recalls hiring a black prostitute in New Orleans, reluctantly, who promised to "do sweet things to me in bed no one had ever done before." "It was flat," however, "and over quickly." He remembers whores from Italy to San Francisco who had made the same promise with the same disappointing results. Even Virginia had sworn as much, and he suspects she could not have delivered if they had gone that far. Only a little more interesting to him are the multiple adulteries he commits with young women from his company and elsewhere; references to these are scattered throughout the monologue. At present he is flirting lasciviously with Jane, a twenty-four-year-old in a neighboring department. He dreads the possibility that she will take him up on one of his bantering invitations; he is certain he can have her whenever he wants, but experience has taught him that what pleasure he may derive will not be worth the complications that may arise afterward. Even his one long-standing extra-marital relationship with a woman named Penny is growing tiresome, although Slocum praises her ability to excite him. She is simply too easy. All his whores and young women are too easy. A number of the latter, he finds, are becoming sexually demanding themselves, many with women's liberation behind them. "Those assertive bitches," he complains. "Generally speaking, I prefer to make *them* do all the doing and giving; that way, I feel I *have* done something to them: I've gotten away with something" (p. 341).

Somewhat oddly, this remark leads to an admission that Virginia frightened him because of her aggressiveness. As much as he wanted/wants her, he confesses that all his desire might well have disappeared had she actually attempted to consummate their flirtation. As with Jane, "I think I enjoyed just *flirting* with her more than anything else: flirting was an end in itself and still often is. I'm still not often sure I really want to get laid" (p. 342). It comes as a surprise when Slocum admits he prefers having sex with his wife. He even admits to fantasizing about her while he's having sex with other women. He spends several pages at the end of the section that concerns her talking about the thrills of their courtship. What he remembers best was being forever in heat with her and looking always for an opportunity to tear off her clothes and go into action. She always responded by attempting unsuccessfully to fight him off, and then submitting, letting him have his way with her while remaining fearfully alert for anyone's approach. "I think now that I probably enjoyed her terror and my violence," Slocum says in a parenthetical aside. He adds:

> I didn't mind that her eyes were open and darting all about and that her strongest emotions were not those of passion or entirely on me, just as long as *I* had her when *I* wanted her and got what *I* wanted; It might, in fact, have added something, that tangy triumphant sense of frenzied danger, that ability to dominate rather than merely persuade, and I often wish I were driven now by that same hectic mixture of blind ardor, haste, and tension. (p. 111)

She is much more excitable and assertive about sex now, especially with daily dips into the bottle. Slocum thinks he liked her better when she was more of a challenge. During one energetic union, his wife cheerfully insists, " 'You made me this way.' " Slocum's rejoinder to the reader is, "I can't believe it was all my fault." Though Slocum rarely says anything without contradicting it somewhere else ("I don't know what I want," he laments in reference to Jane and

Virginia.), one can readily conclude from the sexual thread lacing throughout the novel that sex for Slocum is merely another front, like the office, for masking his fears and insecurity with displays of potency. His sexual activity is rooted not in passion or pleasure, but in his need to exercise power over others.

Something analogous controls his relationships with the members of his family. Slocum has three children, two of them, like his wife, unnamed: a daughter approaching sixteen, a nine-year-old son, and a younger boy, named Derek, who is retarded and will never advance past the mental age of five. We learn something of the first in the section "My daughter is unhappy" and, as usual, much about Slocum.

Slocum initially describes his daughter with a list of adjectives: "lonely," "disgruntled," "unhappy," "dissatisfied," "clever," "malicious," "morose," "rude," "mean," and "depressed." A little later he calls her "nervous, spiteful, embittered, and vindictive." Slocum responds to her occasional subtle cries for help with sardonic wisecracks, a practice he is not proud of but which he claims he cannot stop. He relegates this perverse compulsion to the same dark part of his soul that wants to kick Kagle's leg, that part that actually enjoys the misfortunes of acquaintances who are worse off than he. "There are things going on inside me," he tells us, "I cannot control and do not admire." The more Slocum analyzes his daughter, the more he finds in her that reminds him of himself. For instance,

> She sits alone in her room for long periods of time doing absolutely nothing but thinking (I sit alone in my study for long periods of time doing absolutely the same thing); and what she likes to think about most is herself; what interests her most is herself; what she broods about most is herself; what she likes to talk about most is herself. She is not much different from me, I suppose. (p. 121)

Most of this section is taken up with various confrontations the daughter elicits, usually at the door of Slocum's study. In the first such, as related by Slocum, she tells her father that she does not care whether he or her mother dies, and that if they get divorced—and she believes they should—she would rather be sent away to boarding school than live with either one of them. Slocum gloats over his ability to "outfox" her in such situations by remaining totally impassive, then calling her bluff or stumping her by giving her wholly unexpected answers. In subsequent dialogues, he undercuts her with sarcasm, joke-making, or simply kicking her out of his room. He is perfectly aware, as his wife keeps reminding him, that his daughter really wants help and attention, but he does not want to be forced to take responsibility for her happiness; he hates her misery as much as he hates everyone and everything that begs for his commiseration. He would much rather win the argument and will go to any lengths to do so, though he secretly detests himself for competing with his fifteen-year-old daughter as though she were his peer. "I'm a shit," he says. "But at least I am a successful one."

Like Slocum, his daughter has a vicious strain of sadism that she can deftly bring into play. At one point, Slocum, in a rare display of feeling toward his emotionally broken girl, puts out his arms to embrace her, even though he knows he risks her turning away "in a taunting, jubilant affront." And she does pull away "with a vicious sneer," leaving him feeling hurt and foolish for having opened himself up. Indeed, at least once Slocum even compares his daughter's ability to consciously hurt him to Green's. And as with Green, "I depend on her. I wanted security from her; I do not get it" (p. 173). Far more common, however, are Slocum's acknowledgments that in her self-pity, discontent, and sadistic craft, she is very much like himself.

The line between Slocum's character and the personalities of his children grows thinner in "My little boy is having difficulties," where he talks about his nine-year-old son. This section, the longest one so far, begins with the child's problems in school, largely resulting from his fear of having to perform for authority figures in front of his peers. Gym gives him particular problems, with public speaking close behind. The gym teacher, Forgione, even frightens Slocum when he visits the school for consultation, not because of anything Forgione does—the teacher seems genuinely concerned about the boy's problems and is eager to make things easier for him—but because Forgione is a figure of authority, like Green and Baron and Mrs. Yerger, the oft-mentioned supervisor of the old accident insurance records office who had terrified the young Slocum with her mere presence.

In by now familiar fashion, Slocum, both consciously and unconsciously, draws parallels between his son and himself. In an episode mentioned earlier, for instance, during an argument with his wife and daughter, Slocum tries to win by throwing a tantrum, during which he editorializes,

> I am still a little boy. I am a deserted little boy I know who will never
> grow older and never change, who goes away and then comes back.
> He is badly bruised and very lonely. He is thin. He makes me sad
> whenever I remember him. He is still alive, yet out of my control.
> This is as much as he ever became. He never goes far and always
> comes back. I can't help him. (p. 145)

He whirls out of the room only to stamp inadvertently on his son. The little boy within has run into the little boy without.

His son is meek, sensitive, lovable, vulnerable, and also usually unhappy. After giving a preliminary catalogue of the boy's many fears and vulnerabilities, Slocum cannot help observing, "When I think of him, I think of me." The child seems hopelessly unfit for society as it is. As Forgione phrases it, "He doesn't have a good competitive spirit . . . . He lacks the true will to win." He so good-naturedly enjoys the co-operative spirit of playing basketball or running relay races, for instance, that he throws the ball to the other team or slows down with merry laughter for his competitors to catch up. Naturally, such behavior draws wrath from his peers and annoyed disbelief from coaches and similar figures of command, much to his paralyzed non-comprehension. The boy's generosity with material things brings him similar grief. On one occasion, he had given a pair of chocolate chip cookies to a boy who merely looked like he wanted them. The other boy ate the first but grew suspicious at the second and ended up running off in angry tears. Slocum's son, as open-hearted as he is, cannot understand what he is doing to upset people. He is also mystified by his parents' insistence that he not give his pennies and nickels away to other children, which he does simply because it makes him feel good. Slocum and his wife talk much about "teaching him a lesson" concerning selfishness, competitiveness, and the other rules of society and free enterprise, though they both boast of his sweetness and generosity to other parents. But as Slocum laments, "The truly disgusting thing about all these platitudinous lessons for getting ahead is that sooner or later they all turn out to be true'' (p. 178).

Slocum, of course, does not share his son's sweetness and generosity; in those respects he more resembles his self-centered, sadistic daughter. What he does share is his son's insecurity and vulnerability. Over and over again Slocum links his boy's fears to his own. For instance, both Slocum and his son fear policemen, probably as archetypal authority figures, though they like having them around for protection. Like Slocum, his son "veers away from cripples" and other symbols of misery, mortality, and human imperfection. A long passage in which Slocum confesses his insecurity while sleeping is followed by the anecdote, repeated later as well, of his son's sneaking into the master bedroom to sleep at the foot of his parents' bed after his tonsils were removed. Slocum recounts several times the pain and nausea he felt seeing his boy wake up from the tonsillectomy reeking of ether and with a crescent of blood under one nostril. He suffers when his son suffers, and as his son dreads some undefinable, inevitable doom, Slocum dreads the same, not only for his son, but for himself. Acknowledging the boy's vulnerability, Slocum fears more than anything else that something horrible is going to happen to him. Symptomatic of these fears are the dreams and daydreams Slocum describes in which his son is missing or dying, such as the following:

> The door [of the subway] closes between us before we can both get on or off together, separating us. Or we are walking together and I turn my head away for an instant, and when I turn back, he is gone. Or I forget about him: he slips my mind: and I remember only afterward, when he is no longer present and has disappeared without a trace from my dream, that he is supposed to be with me. I am unable to guess where he has gone. There is only void. I feel lonely then, and it is not possible to be certain which one of us has been lost. I feel lost too. (p. 217)

In another, Slocum dreams that the maid calls him at work and repeats again and again the line, "Mr.———, your boy is lying on the floor of the living room and hasn't breathed for fifteen seconds." Slocum's son, it seems, is the only human being whom he cares about more than himself: "I know I fear for his safety more than I fear for my own, and this surprises me . . . . When he's scared, I'm scared, even though I'm not scared of what he's scared of" (pp. 319-320). He adds a little later, "I have this constant fear something is going to happen to him." He even wishes the boy would "hurry up and get it over with already so I could relax and stop brooding about it in such recurring suspense" (p. 321).

This close identification with his son leads to some curious and revealing passages. In the midst of recalling one dreary summer when the boy had ostracized himself from a day camp, Slocum digresses to the memory of his mother's long, lingering death in a hospital. From there he digresses to fears of his own lingering death somewhere in the future. He concludes by saying, "I cannot help feeling sorry for myself. I cannot help feeling sorry for him." This statement is ambiguous; as the novel progresses Slocum often refers to the insecure little boy inside himself, and in pathetic terms; for instance: "And hiding inside of me somewhere, I know (I feel him inside me. I feel it beyond all doubt), is a timid little boy just like my son who wants to be his best friend and wishes he could come outside and play" (p. 213). Elsewhere he confesses with comparable pathos, "I know at last what I want to be when I grow up. When I grow up I want to be a little boy" (p. 319).

As Slocum's daughter mirrors the sadistic, competitive side of Slocum's personality and his son the vulnerable, insecure side, so does Derek, the idiot son, manifest an aspect of the narrator as well. This connection is not as extensively developed as the others, in large part because Slocum prefers to push this child's existence into the background. "We would prefer not to think about him," he notes parenthetically at the beginning of a chapter devoted to the boy. "We don't want to talk about him." What is psychologically interesting about this chapter, revealingly entitled "It is not true," is that it deals mostly with personality traits of his own that Slocum would just as soon deny.

Initially, there are some superficial comparisons drawn in this chapter between Slocum and this son. Slocum refers to himself as "a feeble-minded idiot" and "a moron" for never having sex with Virginia. Slocum makes much of the idiot boy's inability to talk, only to note later that aggressive women, such as Virginia and Penny, reduce him to moronic speechlessness ("Penny diminishes me into a gargling, babbling imbecile every time."). Far more significant, however, are Slocum's references to his inadequacies, inabilities, sins, and failures. He talks at length about being dominated by his penis, which he considers a mindless, uncontrollable organ, a man's "weakest reed." He discusses further his mother's degeneration and her ultimate reduction to imbecility before her death and speculates again about the same inevitability befalling him. This leads to a passage of striking relevance:

> I can picture such scenes of myself in a nursing home easily enough. I can picture Derek out front easily too, slobbering, a thick-set, clumsy, balding, dark-haired retarded adult male with an incriminating resemblance to a secret me I know I have inside me and want nobody else ever to discover, an inner visage. (p. 366).

From here Slocum shifts to his barely suppressed rage at Kagle, his desire to kick his crippled leg, to strangle him, to mock him mercilessly for being gauche and disgusting, for "having failed." Remembering Slocum's propensity for unconsciously imitating Kagle, one justly concludes that what he dislikes most about Kagle is the latter's embodiment of what Slocum fears he could become: a social embarrassment, an obvious failure, a cripple in more ways than one. Slocum attributes such violent compulsions to his id, as it lusts and hates and struggles against his social self for expression. He is conscious of many beings inside himself, both human and subhuman:

> I am infiltrated and besieged, the unprotected target of sneaky attacks from within. Things stir, roll over slowly in my mind like black eels, and drop from consciousness into inky depths. Everything is smaller. It's neither warm nor cold. There is no moisture. Smirking faces go about their nasty deeds and pleasures surreptitiously without confiding in me . . . . I am infested with ghostlike figures (now you see them, now you don't), with imps and little demons. They scratch and stick me. (p. 373).

Shortly thereafter, he envisions a dream-like Thanksgiving dinner in which his entire family forms a frozen frieze around the table, mapping out the progress of his life.

from mute beginning (Derek) to mute, fatal, bovine end (Mother), passive and submissive as a cow, and even beyond through my missing father (Dad). I am an illustrated flow chart. I have my wife, my daughter, and my son for reference: I am all their ages. They are me. (p. 375)

In this scheme, then, Derek represents Slocum's infantile self—his id/idiot self—that which he yearns to keep most hidden. The specter of Derek stands always in the back of Slocum's psyche, incarnating his terror of genuinely losing control over himself, like Martha, the typist who is going crazy, or Hoiloway, the salesman who everyone knows is heading for his next nervous breakdown, or Kagle, Ed Phelps, or Red Parker, who have become too embarrassing to the company to be allowed to remain. It is this element of social embarrassment that binds Derek, these co-workers, the "Derek in Slocum", and even Slocum's dying, deteriorating mother. Slocum feels desperately the need to "fit in," to conform, to avoid standing out in any unpleasant way. It is this that keeps him from actually kicking Kagle's leg or giving in to the other unseemly impulses that plague him. Slocum worries a great deal about losing this particular battle:

I don't want to go crazy. I like to keep tight rein on my reason, thoughts, and actions, and to know always which is which. I don't want to lose my inhibitions. I might hit people if I did (strangers, friends, and loved ones), commit murder, spout hatred and bigotry, scratch eyeballs, molest teen-age girls and younger ones with trim figures, come on crowded subway trains against the side of a hefty buttock on someone like my wife or Penny. (p. 427)

He even worries that he "might start stuttering." The association of speech defects with madness is significant. According to Heller himself,

Slocum is very conscious of speech. For him it's a concentrate for all forms of potency, including sexual potency. Slocum wants to make a three-minute speech; he's wounded because he's denied it. The one symptom given of the retarded child is that the child doesn't speak. Slocum has a fear early of talking to people who stutter because he may start to stutter too. (From an unpublished interview.)

At the beginning of this novel, Slocum appears painstakingly careful about his choice of words and the ordering of the narrative, even to interpolating parenthetical corrections of his own grammar. By the time the monologue reaches the section "It is not true," however, the rigidity of Slocum's prose has disintegrated. Most obvious is the indiscriminate use of parentheses, sometimes enclosing digressions that go on for a page or more, some containing parenthetical digressions of their own. Related to this idiosyncrasy is Slocum's difficulty in the latter part of the book to remain with one topic for more than, or even as long as, a paragraph. Not infrequently, the reader finds himself following a disquisition on one subject, only to come up against a concluding sentence about something completely different, as when Slocum ends a paragraph concering Derek's future as a retarded adult with the line, "I hope I don't find out my wife is committing adultery, even though she probably should" (p. 425).

And of course there are the endless repetitions, the direct contradictions ("And they would be right./ And they would be wrong."), and the echolalia of the increasingly compulsive "Ha, ha" that follows every bit of black and dubious humor, e.g., "[Derek] begins with certain congenital handicaps that are impossible for me to overcome. (Ha, ha.)" (p. 424). The evidence suggests that Slocum may be disintegrating along with his prose, that he may be following Martha and Holloway toward a complete breakdown.

Slocum's dread of the irrational becomes frantic with the opening of the next section, "There's no getting away from it." "I've got to get rid of him and don't know how," he says, referring to Derek and by extension to what Derek represents in his own psyche. "There's no one I can even tell I want to, not even my wife . . . . " A page later he complains, "I have conversations that do not seem to be mine," then goes on to describe feeling abstracted from his legs, from his headaches, from segments of his personal history, from discussions at the office. "Is this schizophrenia," he wonders, "or merely a normal, natural, typical, wholesome, logical, universal schizoid formation?" (p. 473)

In these chapters that begin with references to Derek, Slocum returns to the question of his insecurity, and glosses it with anecdotes. One of particular interest concerns his wife. Slocum worries about her committing adultery, although he is sure she would not. He finds himself examining her body and her clothes at the most unlikely times for marks of infidelity. He fears the possibility of actually discovering something that will force him to act. "I have something more potent than an ordinary hypocritical, male chauvinist double standard to give me the strength and determination to walk out," he adds; "I have insecurity" (p. 429). We learn of other methods he has for asserting a competitive edge over his wife, such as refusing to tell her he loves her and not waking her up when she's having a nightmare. Such behavior, looked at closely, also turns out to be rooted in his insecurity; he wants to keep "the whammy" on his wife and prevent her from becoming a threat to him.

"In the family in which I live there are four people of whom I am afraid," Slocum proclaims in a paraphrase of his statement regarding his company. "Three of these four people are afraid of me, and each of these three is also afraid of the other two. Only one member of the family is not afraid of any of the others, and that one is an idiot" (p. 333).

By the latter part of the novel, the only character that Slocum feels comfortable with is Arthur Baron; not only is Baron a substitute father figure, by the narrator's own admission, he offers Slocum security and even potency in the form of the promotion to Kagle's job. When the advancement finally occurs, however, it seems on most fronts a pyrrhic victory. His wife is disgusted with him for betraying Kagle, his office colleagues mistrust him, and he remembers at this time that his mother's last words to him were, "You're no good."

The last two chapters are brief, together about 38 pages long. At the beginning of the first of these, "My boy has stopped talking to me." Slocum relates with obvious pain his son's rejection of him. The boy remains silent and suspicious and shuts Slocum off by keeping his bedroom door closed. The family's moral center, the boy is apparently distressed with his father for replacing Kagle, as well as frightened that he, being as vulnerable, could be gotten rid of as easily. Slocum's daughter, morose because he will not let her have a car, also remains behind closed doors, leading Slocum to complain that at home "things are going inexorably out of control. Things are not out of control at the office," on the other hand, and it is there, where he is learning to wield his new potency—even to taunting Jack Green a little—that he prefers to spend his time. He still worries, nevertheless, about his mortality, about wanting to divorce his wife and get rid of Derek, about his daughter and son drifting away from him, and about losing his mind and his self-control.

It is at this point that the reader slams up against the most disturbing, disorienting, and critically controversial moment in the narrative. Something happens: Slocum finds his son cut, bleeding, and screaming on the sidewalk, the victim of a car accident. He enfolds the boy in his arms and smothers him to death. It all takes place in half a page. When he finds out the child had been only superficially injured, his first remark is, "Don't tell my wife."

There are at least two critical protests raised regarding this episode. First, it happens so fast that, to paraphrase Nelson Algren, it is practically a non-event. Second, it supplies a false climax, unprepared for and leaving unresolved basic conflicts of the novel. On the first reading, both these complaints seem justified. But a subsequent perusal of the text uncovers a number of foreshadowings of this event. In one of the boy's first appearances, Slocum is "pulverizing him beneath the crushing weight of my overwhelming solicitude," to which remark is appended, "I can't seem to help him, I do seem to harm him" (p. 146). Over and over Slocum expresses the dread that "something bad is going to happen to him" and prays only that when it does Slocum will be dead and "no longer . . . harmed by whatever tragedy it is that pains and cripples him severely (I can't stand pain) or strikes him down fatally" (p. 213). "I have the recurring fear," he says elsewhere, "that he will die before I do." He also expresses several times a fear of automobiles ("I don't trust cars. God knows who may be driving the ones close enough to collide with us." p. 233), and in particular the fear of losing his boy to one. At another point, confronted with his son's utter helplessness, Slocum states, "I wanted to kill him . . . then I wanted to clasp him to me lovingly and protectively . . . ." (p. 315). There are too many such remarks for them to be anything less than pointed hints.

One must bear in mind as well what the boy represents: Slocum's insecurity and fear—of mortality, pain, isolation, authority, and responsibility. Ironically, and somewhat chillingly, Slocum manages to pull himself completely together after smothering his son. In the last five pages of the novel, we see Slocum functioning as a competent, confident, responsible executive and family man. He has gotten over his insecurity, and in its absence told his wife he loves her, given his daughter a car, and decided to keep Derek home after all. He has finally made his speech at the company convention. He has stood up to Green and the belligerent Johnny Brown. He has eased out of his department the company embarrassments—Kagle, Phelps, and Parker. The worst has even happened: Martha, the typist, has finally gone crazy on the job, a situation Slocum handles with immense aplomb. The novel ends on this scene with the line, "Everyone seems pleased with the way I've taken command." Only once in the chapter does Slocum allude to his son, with the brief sentence, tucked into the middle of a paragraph, "I miss my boy." Slocum has smothered with his son the phobias that were unbalancing his mind. By taking command of his son's death, he has brought about "the inevitable" with his own hands. He has confronted his worse fears and overcome them; he has killed the frightened boy in himself. What is of course hideous about this resolution is that Slocum's successful self-healing is the result of an act of homocide. Slocum has repressed his responsibility for the death by keeping the reference to it brief; even in his "healthier" state, he remains unattractive. But at least, to paraphrase him, he is a *successful* shit.

As Nelson Algren noted, it is difficult to tell how the author feels about this character. Heller himself has said that for most of the book he found Slocum contemptible, but by the end he felt sorry for him. In fact, Slocum does have moments of genuine pathos, moving in their universal application to the human condition, as when he muses on the trauma of birth in a passage that ends,

> I was in need of whatever nipple succored me and whatever arms
> uplifted me. I didn't know names. I loved the food that fed me—
> that's all I knew—and the arms that held and hugged and turned me
> and gave me to understand, at least for those periods, that I was not
> alone and someone else knew I was there. Without them, I would
> have been alone. (p. 522)

Slocum's fears by and large are the fears of most men in this society at this time—fears of death, the loss of loved ones, loss of potency, loss of job and social status, loss of social acceptability, etc. Slocum finds himself in a world in which everyone is afraid of everyone else, at home as at work, in which there is no comfort in love or love-making, no comfort but only boredom and fear, "no water but only rock." This is the world of Eliot's *The Waste Land*, in which there are no ideals that work and no values worth working for, in which everyone finds time dragging on his/her hands—time Slocum tries to use up in empty, unsatisfying womanizing—and the most frequent complaint heard is "I have nothing to do": nothing meaningful to do with one's life, nothing to do to make the world better or to make a mark on it. Cause and effect barely exist in this environment: when Slocum contemplates mutilating his paycheck card to see what would happen, he realizes morosely that nothing would happen—"I can no longer change the environment or even disturb it seriously." Elsewhere he observes, "A man was shot in the park today. Nobody knows why." Indeed, in smothering his son Slocum finally takes cause and effect by the throat and makes something happen.

If this world does not seem exactly like the one we all know, it comes meta-phorically close; as in *Catch-22*, Heller has held a fish-eye lens to reality that exaggerates and distorts the image it brings into focus. Slocum's world is the postwar world of material success, the nuclear family, and the American Dream, except that success is pointless and unfulfilling, an end in itself, the family a nest of hatreds, fears, and suspicions, and the American Dream a nightmare in gray worsted. In a society that operates by the ethic of competition and personal ambition, every human being finds himself always wanting more than he can ever have, and always, ultimately, alone in a never-ending struggle with everybody else as with a host of forces he can neither understand nor control.

The relentless bleakness of this novel, then, reflects the inherent emptiness Heller sees in the values of postwar American society. Again, as in *Catch-22* and *We Bombed in New Haven*, he has given us a work about moral choice, in which the only alternatives are desperate ones. Slocum, following Starkey rather than Yossarian, opts for the values by which society operates, achieving success by its ruthless standards, but at the cost of killing a part of himself. If *Something Happened* is not as funny as the earlier works—and it definitely is not—it is because, as Heller has observed, Slocum is not funny. Neither is the fictive world he inhabits and the society he typifies.

Carefully read, *Something Happened* proves to be a hard-hitting condemnation of American life in our times. Unfortunately, few readers will have the patience to read the book so carefully. The rhetorical and artistic obstacles Heller sets up therein are all but insurmountable. The narrator himself, despite his moments of pathos, is at times intolerable and fundamentally impossible to identify with. While the prose is sprinkled with a number of witty turns of phrase, puns, and frequent ironies, it contains virtually nothing in the way of humor. The repetitiousness, like the humorlessness, may have an artistic basis in Slocum's obsessive personality, but it is excruciating and even tiresome to read. As one reviewer put it, *Something Happened* is "a teeth-gritting literary experience" (*Library Journal*, 15 March 1979, p. 752). It is one of those books that must be studied, and not merely read, to be appreciated.

IV:
GOOD AS GOLD

Only five years passed between the publication of *Something Happened* and Heller's next—and most recent— novel, *Good as Gold*, in 1979. The relative proximity of these two works, contrasted with the twelve-year span that separated *Something Happened* from *Catch-22*, may be due in part to a factor not usually considered in connection with serious art, but mentioned publicly by Heller on more than one occasion. He has tied the length of time it took him to finish *Something Happened* to his income from *Catch-22*; in short, as long as his first novel was earning substantial sums, he did not need to publish a second. Since *Something Happened* did not do anywhere near as well with the buying public, Heller may have been motivated to turn out his third novel somewhat more quickly.

Another reason, and perhaps a more important one, was the novel's timeliness. *Good as Gold* is ostensibly a satire directed at our politicians and political institutions; it belongs to the Seventies, to the Watergate era, when virtually everyone across the philosophical spectrum had (and still has) some reason to be disgusted with the political process. *Good as Gold*, at the same time, is Heller's most personal work. While *Catch-22* grew out of Heller's World War II experiences and *Something Happened* borrowed from his work in advertising, *Good as Gold* goes all the way back to Heller's roots in the Jewish quarter of Coney Island, which he shares with the likes of Mel Brooks and Woody Allen; indeed, Heller numbers Brooks among his oldest friends.

Bruce Gold is Heller's first Jewish protagonist (although more than one reviewer noted Jewish traits in the WASP narrator of *Something Happened*). In the first two short sections of the novel, the reader is introduced to Gold's inner circle: his two closest friends and his family. The first section, "The Jewish Experience," features his friends, Pomoroy and Lieberman. Pomoroy is the serious, cynical executive editor of a publishing company. Lieberman has satisfied his college ambition of managing a small intellectual magazine, but now wants much more and is willing to stoop to anything to get it. He is almost wholly unattractive: fat, balding, pompous, self-centered, whining, hypocritical, ambitious far beyond his capabilities, and envious of the successes of his friends. He is forever the butt of their jibes and tolerates them only because no one else will have him around. Gold himself is a college English professor who remains in print by writing articles of topical interest. In this first chapter, we discover he is contemplating doing a book on "the Jewish Experience in America," which leads to an exchange between the three men that smacks more of the ruthless code of business than of friendly affection. Mention is also made of a phone call Gold received from Ralph Newsome, a former

WASP classmate of his who is now on the White House staff, in response to a semi-favorable review Gold wrote of a book composed by the President.

The two worlds of the novel—New York Jewry and Washington—are developed further in the next short section, "My Year in the White House," named for the President's book. Here the reader first meets Gold's family, initially his older sisters: the doting Rose and Esther, the officious school teacher Ida, and the morose, stingey, chain-smoking Muriel, as well as their respective mates. Soon encountered, and dominating the family scene, are Gold's older brother Sid and his bitter wife Harriet, his mad stepmother, and the family patriarch, his contrary, tyrannical old father. The conversations that take place at the frequent, and to Gold detestable, family dinners sound in their general abusiveness and irrationality like something out of *Alice in Wonderland*. Usually Gold finds himself being ineffectively praised and defended by his sisters and by Belle, his stable, patient wife, while the object of the wrathful scorn of his father, the weird insults of his stepmother, and the heavy-handed teasing of his brother. Sid is particularly fond of bringing up a bit of misinformation that only he and Gold know is wrong, challenging him to start an argument he cannot win with the more gullible members of the family. Even Gold's usually helpful sisters and usually silent in-laws tend to side with the older Sid in these cases. A typical, humorous example is the following, in which Sid, with malice aforethought, has implied that north is in fact "up." When Gold incredulously asks Sid, "Do you really think something is higher just because it's north?" the entire family, in-laws and all, attacks back:

> "Of course, it's higher. They got the mountains there, don't they?"
> "That's why people go in the summer."
> "It's cooler."
> "North is always higher on the map," Ida pointed out.
> "I'm not talking about a map."
> "That's why the water always flows down to the middle of the map," said his father with belittling arrogance. "Where it's wider. Where there's lots of room."
> "And I suppose," Gold sneered at them all, "that if you took a map off the wall and turned it upside down, all the water would run off."
> "Oh, no, silly," said his sister-in-law.
> "There's no water on a map."
> "He thinks there's water on a map."
> "A map is only a picture."
> "I know it's a picture!" Gold shrieked in fear. "I was being ironic. I was asking a question, not making a statement!" (p. 109; all citations are from the Pocket Books edition [New York, 1979])

More vicious are the repeated attacks Gold suffers from his father. No matter what Gold says or does, his father finds something wrong with it. His major complaint is that Gold, the successful academic and author, has no "business sense," unlike Sid, who runs a company that manufactures laundry machines. This accusation is particularly ironic coming from a man who failed in every trade he ever tried, and several times in his chosen profession, tailoring. Gold once remembers his father calling him across the street only to introduce him to a group of men as "my son's brother . . . the one who never amounted to anything." At times the old man can be monstrously cruel, not only to Gold but to his sisters. Generally, however, he is merely vociferously cranky and contrary. At its most basic level, this contrariness manifests itself in an absurd exchange between him and Gold:

> "Let's go to Lundy's," he suggested. "It's right here. We'll have a good piece of fish."
> "What's so good about it?" said his father.
> "So"—Gold declined to argue—"it won't be so good."
> "Why you getting me fish that's no good?"
> "Black," said Gold.
> "White," said his father.
> "White," said Gold.
> "Black," said his father.
> "Cold."
> "Warm."
> "Tall."
> "Short."
> "Short."
> "Tall."
> "I'm glad," said Gold, "you remember your game."
> "Who says it's a game?" (pp. 94-95)

The father is also prone to a number of idiosyncrasies, one being his violent refusal to be served anything in cracked or chipped china, leading to one very messy scene in a restaurant.

The demented stepmother is contrary in her own peculiar way and contradicts not only the rest of the family but herself as well; she also has her own set of idiosyncrasies. For instance:

> She was always knitting thick white wool. When he complimented her once on her knitting, she informed him with a flounce that she was crocheting. When he inquired next time how her crocheting was going she answered, "I don't crochet. I knit." Often she called him to her side just to tell him to move away. Sometimes she came up to him and said, "Cackle, cackle." (p. 19)

Every time Gold sees her, he observes, she "loses another marble." At times her mindlessness even outrages Gold's father, as when she wonders aloud at one family dinner where he would like to be buried when he dies. Despite his vehement refusal to discuss the subject, she persists, driving the whole family into a lunatic exchange regarding burial plots, in which Gold, as he does elsewhere, loses track of the voices and begins assigning them to fictional characters like old Karamazov, Lady Chatterley, Twemlow, and Cinderella. "So many people," he laments at one point about his family. "And all of them strange."

Gold's intercourse with the other Jews of his neighborhood crowd spans the same spectrum from heavyhanded ribbing to outright cruelty. Dr. Murray Weinrock, for instance, an old acquaintance who is now Gold's physician, unsparingly plays practical jokes on him during examinations, while Murray's brother Spotty trades insults with Gold at the YMCA gymnasium while avoiding the payment of an $1100 debt. It is finally evident that in the pecking order established during Gold's childhood, Gold finds himself only one step above the universally detested Lieberman. As Spotty Weinrock reveals in one place to Gold's chagrin, everyone thought Gold a schmuck then and everyone continues to regard him as a schmuck. In his Jewish subculture, anyway, Gold has good reason to complain (with comedian Rodney Dangerfield) that he gets no respect, not even from his smart-aleck twelve-year-old daughter.

By contrast, the world of Washington, D.C., represented largely by Ralph Newsome, shows Gold exaggerated esteem. Coming immediately after the first family dinner described in the novel, Newsome's first conversation with Gold reveals that the White House is impressed with Gold's ability to coin phrases, in this case "contemporary universal constituency," and is considering him for a government position. Newsome's most characteristic trait—it is soon clear—is self-contradiction. The following bit of their first dialogue is typical:

> "What would I have to do?" [Gold asked.]
>
> "Anything you want, as long as it's everything we tell you to say and do in support of our policies, whether you agree with them or not. You'll have complete freedom."
>
> Gold was confused. He said delicately, "I can't be bought, Ralph."
>
> "We wouldn't want you if you could be, Bruce," Ralph responded. "This President doesn't want yes-men. What we are want are independent men of integrity who will agree with all our decisions after we make them. You'll be entirely on your own." (p. 50)

Where such self-contradiction appears elsewhere in the novel—notably in the speech of Gold's crazy stepmother—as elsewhere in Heller's work, it signifies the inversion of reason and, more broadly, the absence of (moral) order. In Newsome's case, however, this rhetorical device is so blatant as to make even meaninglessness seem meaningless. Ralph's pronouncements continue to be mutually negating and completely empty. Also fairly empty are the phrases of Gold's he enthusiastically grabs and circulates in Washington, catch-phrases such as "You're boggling my mind" and the only slightly more meaningful "Nothing succeeds as planned" and "Every change is for the worse." The ultimate along these lines is reached when, later, to a journalist's question, Gold responds, "I don't know," and the remark immediately becomes *de rigeur* in government circles, from the President on down.

All further conversations between Gold and Newsome run just the same way, with Newsome promising Gold positions—even, significantly, Secretary of State—but saying essentially nothing and occasionally picking up another relatively vacuous phrase that Gold comes up with and passing it on to Washington officialdom. Newsome also, however, establishes the connection, found as well in *Something Happened*, between sexual potency and power in general, in demonstration of Kissinger's statement, quoted more than once in the novel, that "power is the ultimate aphrodisiac." For instance, when Gold first visits Newsome's office, he finds Ralph surrounded by beautiful and willing receptionists and secretaries. Frequent references follow to the prominence of promiscuity in government circles, and Gold at one point torments Lieberman by telling him that all he does in Washington is "fuck girls." By this time Gold, through Newsome, has been re-introduced to a former acquaintance, Andrea

Conover, heiress of the WASP Establishment, the sole progeny of Pugh Biddle Conover, a wealthy, aristocratic old "kingmaker" who, according to Ralph, can help Gold get a good position with the government if Gold will divorce Belle and marry Andrea. The idea appeals to Gold, and upon his first meeting with Andrea they begin an affair.

Andrea is everything Gold's wife is not: tall, blond, stunning, rich, and not the least domestic. During their various trysts in Washington, Gold finds himself enthralled with her beauty and her admiration of him; he also finds himself doing all of the cooking and cleaning. Eventually he discovers he is growing bored, as well as appalled at Andrea's approach to love and sexuality. For instance, she talks freely to associates, even to her father, about the intimacies of her relationship with Gold. She also, much to Gold's distress, relates to him her wide range of sexual experiences with other men, some of which smack of sado-masochism and incest. Some weeks after their engagement—though Gold still hasn't separated from Belle—he finds her preparing to spend a weekend with another man. Her response to his suppressed outrage is completely ingenuous; she maintains that the other man is only going to have her body and states, innocently, "maybe I won't give it away any more after we're married." Drawing more closely the parallel between sexuality and power is Gold's response:

> Not for this, he told himself, was he leaving his wife, provoking the enmity of his children, offending his family, and forsaking for the time all other erotic relationships, but for money, beauty, social position, political preference, and a stupendous magnification of sexual prestige . . . . (p. 249).

The sort of moral laxness that Andrea embodies is characteristic of the non-Jewish world depicted herein. In fact, as Joanie, Gold's younger sister who lives in Beverly Hills, tells him that is how she and her husband avoid being Jewish: "We screw around, commit adultery, and talk out loud a lot about fucking."

In the last-mentioned confrontation with Andrea, Gold does succeed in "reasserting his supremacy over her," and they end up heading for her father's estate for the weekend so that Gold can meet Pugh Biddle Conover.

Conover stands at the summit of the WASP Establishment; his wealth and position go back almost as far as the nation itself. Gold finds the man clean, dapper, and initially admirable, and does his best to please him. He soon discovers, however, that the old man is not only openly/anti-Semitic, but as obnoxious and demented in his way as Gold's father and stepmother together. He accuses Gold, among other things, of being a pushy, social-climbing Jew and asserts, with some justification, that in marrying Andrea he is merely "choosing a wife appropriate for the new career in Washington toward which you presently think you are directed." While he expresses an admiration for Gold's work, like all the representatives of the WASP Establishment, he has none at all for Gold.

Conover's reaction to Gold resembles that of another powerful WASP figure in the novel: the character called simply "the Governor." A political wheeler-dealer from Texas reminiscent of Lyndon Johnson and John Connally, he heads a commission to which Gold has been assigned, a commission with no apparent role but to meet periodically so that its two dozen members can draw exorbitant salaries from the government. In conversation with Gold, the Governor boasts

of all the "peckers in his pocket," an affirmation of his political power para-
phrased from a statement attributed at the front of the book to LBJ. The Governor, like Conover, makes much of Gold's Jewishness, but offers to help him in
Washington provided Gold keeps his place. Gold demonstrates, by fawning,
that he is willing to do just that. At the end of this scene comes this apostrophe
from Gold:

> . . . oh, the joy—the intoxicating ecstasy of being insulted and con-
> descended to by people of established social position who ignored,
> abused, or despised him, the gratification in being admitted into
> such company as an insignificant status-seeker to be overlooked and
> snubbed, interrupted when he did try to speak and banished with
> such grace from each conversation he attempted to penetrate . . . .
> How he envied their sense of belonging and their impervious stu-
> pidity. (p. 214)

Despite the ironic tone of this passage, we are forced to assume that the irony
in this case is the narrator's and not Gold's. Gold is not, in fact, particularly
admirable in his dealings with the WASP-Washington power structure. In this
respect, he resembles the other Jews in the novel who have significant ties with
the Establishment or desire them. At the low end of this spectrum lies Lieberman, who is doing everything he can to insinuate himself into political circles,
mostly by writing jingoistic editorials militantly supporting the Administration's
positions. He disgusts Pomoroy and Gold with his willingness to be identified
with reactionaries and even neo-fascists, and for his ready hypocrisy. As
Lieberman once declares, in representative fashion, "I don't think they appre-
ciate how loyal I can be. I can switch positions overnight on any issue they want
me to" (p. 168).

Another Jew from the old neighborhood who *has* succeeded is Harris Rosenblatt. An economist, Rosenblatt has caught the admiration of the Establishment with a meaningless catch-phrase of his own: "balance the budget."
In fact he is so much a part of WASP circles now that he has physically meta-
morphosed; he is no longer a short, plump, slightly epicene Semite—as Gold
remembers him—but tall, lean, and definitely Teutonic of face and feature.
"I used to be Jewish," he tells Gold at one point. Like Newsome, Rosenblatt
speaks almost wholly in cliches and empty phrases. He is apparently a personal
friend of Pugh Conover's, although we learn soon that Conover considers him
another upstart and amuses himself at Rosenblatt's unwitting expense, convincing him, for instance, to shoot his "best dog" under the guise of tradition after
a successful hunt.

Though Gold disparages both colleagues, he himself is guilty of similar
crimes; he fawns, for example, not just with Conover and the Governor, but
even with Newsome. Gold appears cognizant of what he is doing but makes no
attempt to change his behavior. Having received the promise of power, there is
apparently little he won't do to bring about its fulfillment, as we have seen,
from leaving his wife to allowing himself to be insulted by anti-Semites. In a
narrative aside that immediately follows Gold's encounter with the Governor,
the reader is informed:

> "Invite a Jew to the White House (and You Make Him Your
> Slave)" was a snide attack on Lieberman he had planned writing

after the latter's invitation to the White House for supporting a war. How close, as Ralph had discerned, Gold often came by whim, jealousy, and blind intuition to the fundamental truths of his world. (p. 214)

Gold's tendencies toward hypocrisy have been evident from early in the novel. One particularly revealing bit of narrative begins with, "Gold was flexible and unopinionated now and able—with just a few minor adjustments in emphasis—to deliver essentially the same speech to an elderly reactionary religious group that he had given the day before with equal success to a congress of teenaged Maoists" (p. 43). It goes on to relate his preference for millionaires and Republicans over less well-funded and influential students and Democrats. At the end of this passage, Gold's ambitions are compared to Lieberman's.

Elsewhere, Gold reveals that he thinks little of his own intellectual honesty as a professor and writer, though he does his best to conceal his doubts from others and fully expects more than the "baffled awe" he gets from his family. In other words, the disrespect he inspires from the other members of his sub-culture somewhat mirrors his own secret self-image; he thus expects others to think more highly of his work than in fact he does himself. Only in his relationship with the Establishment does he succeed in convincing, and then it is only his work and not his person that receives the respect.

Gold himself is amazed at the earnestness with which his words are received by officialdom. For instance, at one point he publishes an article in the New York *Times* entitled "Education and Truth *or* Truth in Education" (from which that section of the novel takes its title). The phone call he gets in response is from a leader in the State Senate who wants Gold's help in "denying financial aid to any community in New York containing poor people." When Gold suggests instead, wryly, that the law be changed to give money only to poor people who live outside the state, the Senator expresses tremendous enthusiasm for the idea. Next Gold receives a call from Ralph, who informs him of the President's approval of Gold's statement that "an ignorant citizen is the best citizen." When Gold tells him that he was being ironic, Ralph replies, "I'm afraid we all missed that, Bruce,' " Gold then observes, " 'Lately . . . all my sarcasms are being received as truths' " (p. 155).

Near the end of the novel, when Spotty Weinrock is telling Gold of his low status in the old neighborhood, he classes Gold among those Jews who got ahead by impressing gentiles and definitely not Jews. Foremost in this group is the real villain of the book and the target of its harshest barbs: Henry Kissinger. He is put forth as the best/worst example of a Jew who has achieved success in Washington and with the WASP power structure in general. The remarks concerning Kissinger begin early in the novel. The first is the mention of a book that Gold is thinking of writing about the former Secretary of State and for which he has been collecting newspaper clippings. The attacks don't really begin, however, until about half-way through the novel, when Gold already has his feet in the fetid pool of Washington and his prospective book on the Jewish experience has turned into his prospective book on Kissinger. At a news conference where the presidential spokesman demonstrates at length the popularity of Gold's emptiest catch-phrase, "I don't know," one journalist begins a series of questions on the Watergate scandal and its aftermath, in which this exchange appears:

"You remember Henry Kisinger, don't you? What was your opinion of him?"

"Second-rate."

"That was his opinion of Richard Nixon, wasn't it?"

"Make that third-rate."

"That's something that's always puzzled me, Ron. If Richard Nixon was second-rate, what in the world *is* third-rate?"

"Henry Kissinger."

"You rate Henry Kissinger *below* Richard Nixon?"

"Only in intelligence and wit. In character and credibility they're about the same." (p. 217)

Further on, the reader comes across other cracks at Kissinger. On pp. 242-243, the narrative repeats a handful of widely circulated jokes about him. At the very beginning of the section "Invite a Jew to the White House (and You Make Him Your Slave)" stands the line: "Bruce Gold still could not understand how any Jew of right mind and good character would have put himself in the services of Richard Nixon, and he could think of none who had." Shortly thereafter, none other than Ralph Newsome remarks, "I distrusted Kissinger from the start and always found him something of a clown." And he goes on: "I have to confess I always thought of Kissinger as a greasy, vulgar, petulant, obnoxious, contemptible, self-serving, social-climbing Jewish little shit" (p. 286). The last six pages of this section almost read like an expository essay on the sins of Kissinger, including at least two pages of quotations from newspaper accounts and editorials. Gold editorializes himself on Kissinger's announced memoirs, questioning the man's ability to do a better job of them than Gold could: "For one thing, he had an objective antipathy toward his subject possibly lacking, or weaker, in Kissinger himself" (pp. 361-362). Heller/Gold berates Kissinger for his unfeeling responsibility for the war in Cambodia, for perpetuating the reign of Richard Nixon, for waging a violent, unjust war in Vietnam and then losing, for working against Israel, for tapping the private telephone lines of his aides, for being evasive, untrustworthy, "full of shit," and so on.

As the novel approaches its climax, the blows at Kissinger aim lower. There is the particularly long, fierce diatribe—liberally sprinkled with Yiddish constructions and *schimpf*-words—that begins with Gold's father screaming, "He ain't no Jew." Excerpts follow:

> The lonesome cowboy was *ba-kokt* again, and it was his allies in South Vietnam who would not accept the *tsedreydt mishmosh* of a truce he had *ungerpotchket*. So, *Moisheh Kapoyer*, the North was bombed to placate the South and salve the hurt feelings of the *mieskeit* and his *umgliks*, and not, as Kissinger falsely indicated, to force new concessions. (p. 385)

> Gold could detect with his nose a rancid tint of swaggering fascism in such arrogant deeds that did not fit flatteringly the plump bourgeois figure who committed them and was not in concordance with even the most prejudicial historic depictions of the characteristic Jew. (p. 382)

This goes on for nearly fifteen pages, again replete with newspaper clippings, after which Gold—having just finished by tracing Kissinger's history of currying the favor of such Anglo-Saxon pillars of society as Rockefeller—seeks out Pugh Conover again to fawn for a favor.

Conover, we soon discover, detests Kissinger as well and refers to him in much the same terms he uses to insult the other politically ambitious Jews in the novel, i.e., Rosenblatt and Gold. Finally, the Governor, that other representative of the WASP power structure, calls Kissinger that "[f]unny-looking fellow with that nose of his and bumblebee mouth." He goes on:

> Had a reputation for backbiting and slanderous remarks about others
> . . . . He's the one who got down on his knees with Nixon to pray to
> God on that rug. Laughed my head off when I heard about that and
> gave a barbecue on my ranch for seventeen thousand people to cele-
> brate. Make war, said Nixon, and he made war. Pray to God, said
> Nixon, and he prayed to God. Seems to me his God was Nixon.
> (p. 469)

Then the Governor relates an incident in which he had, in essence, told Kissinger in strong, patronizing, and insulting terms to keep in his place, after which, the Governor says, "I knew I had his pecker in my pocket." He introduces these remarks with the statement, "every Jew should have a big gentile for a friend, and every successful American should own a Jew" (p. 469).

The negative comments concerning Kissinger made by such representatives of the Establishment as Newsome, Conover, and the Governor could be taken as evidence of their anti-Semitism were it not that they are seconded by Spotty Weinrock, by Gold's father, and primarily by Gold himself. This universal distaste for Kissinger seems to belie Spotty's assertion that Jews who are not popular with Jews tend to be popular with gentiles. Despite his success with the WASP Establishment, Kissinger appears to be popular with no one. This contradiction cannot be explained within the context of the novel; it seems to be a case of Heller's admitted personal dislike of Kissinger intruding upon the esthetic coherence of his materials.

Kissinger's prominence around the novel's climax does bring together the dual themes of politics and the "Jewish experience." Regarding the latter, Gold has continued his background research among his older siblings and neighborhood acquaintances, learning much about the very real anti-Semitism they had experienced in the first decades of the century and of the difficulties of survival during the Depression. Particularly during one long lunchtime discussion with Sid, the reader experiences a level of genuine affection not otherwise obvious in the dealings between Jews in the novel, even between members of the same family. Through his potential connection with the government, Gold also meets Greenspan, an FBI agent assigned to keep an eye on him, who in fact acts, in the latter part of the plot, as an orthodox Jewish conscience, forever present in some ghostly fashion and forever warning Gold away from his adulteries and other defections from Mosaic law and tradition with the frequent admonition, "You're a *shonda* to your race."

Greenspan is present as Gold, near the novel's end, reaches the ultimate in Anglo-Saxon decadence by suddenly, carnally falling in love with his daughter's teacher, one Linda Book, and attempting to take both her and Andrea on a long, sexually energetic weekend in Acapulco. Gold mentally lives through this weekend, while it is still in planning, as he tortures himself with his usual eight laps at the YMCA. The frenetic, madcap activity of the prospective orgy, in which Gold pictures himself running from one woman to the other while commencing an intensely physical flirtation with a Mexican actress, alternates with distractions in the gym, particularly the taunts of Spotty Weinrock, who though fat and out of condition appears to be passing Gold repeatedly on the track. Greenspan darts in and out of the fantasy, lamenting Gold's behavior. Eventually, amid the exhausting reveries, Gold sees that Spotty is playing another nasty trick on him, hiding in the corners of the gym and then running out to pass him as he comes by. At his moment of greatest rage, he stumbles and hits the track with a pain in his chest that has all the marks of a heart attack. His last words to Spotty as he is carted into the ambulance are, "Tell not a soul." A heartbeat away from death," Gold suddenly realizes, "and his dominant concern was not life, but that corrupting illusion of triumph, public success" (p. 450).

Gold learns his real relationship to both his overlapping worlds—i.e., his true isolation—when no one misses him during his ten-day stay in the hospital. Neither Belle nor Andrea, both of whom he phones upon his discharge, knew where he was or particularly cared. The only one who did know, Spotty Weinrock, had forgotten. Linda Book was the most concerned by his absence, but only because Gold has been paying her children's dental bills. He discovers at this time, incidentally, that she shares Andrea's vice for telling everyone about their sex life, and that as a result her estranged husband is cutting off all financial support and gunning for him. Gold appeals to the ubiquitous Greenspan to save him; Greenspan succeeds, mournfully insisting yet again that Gold is a *shonda*, "no worse than the rest [in Washington] . . . but certainly no better."

Following these false climaxes, the real turning point comes in the next chapter when Gold gets an invitation to the Embassy Ball where, he has been assured, he will finally meet the President and get his government appointment. The instant Gold enters the ball, however, he receives a long-distance call from his sister Ida informing him that Sid has died of a heart attack. Gold's initial reaction is a callous, "He does this to me every time. He'll ruin my whole day, my whole weekend." But family ties end up outweighing Gold's political ambitions, and he leaves the ball for home, albeit reluctantly.

Sid's funeral is the ultimate mixture of mutual dislike and affection between the members of Gold's family. The abusiveness remains, though subdued. Gold's farewell to his brother is a screamed, " 'Sid, you fuck—why did you have to die? Who will take care of us now?' " "But no one heard," the narrative adds; "His words were smothered in sobs" (p. 475). Afterwards, he finds his father utterly dispirited and pathetic and finds himself the moral head of the family. A cranky, relatively mild insult from the old man settles "amidst the various other corrosive recollections of recent origins that were seething in his brain with such depressing and infuriating effect: Ralph would not hide him, Conover would taunt him, the ex-Governor of Texas owned him" (p. 480). Gold suddenly decides to refuse any role with the government.

The funeral observations wind down with Greenspan a major participant, as Gold cuts his connections with Ralph and binds himself to his family. Gold abandons the book on Kissinger and reverts to the original one on the Jewish experience. He embraces his Judaism by paying his respects at the grave of his mother, then witnesses a droll scene at a Jewish religious school, where a group of boys in *yarmulkas* and sidelocks are arguing and sulking in the middle of a baseball game being played in the dead of winter. A "stiff-necked, contrary people," Gold muses affectionately, still wondering how to begin to write about them. On this note, the novel ends.

Looked at closely, the rapid climactic events that unravel the plot leave a number of loose ends in the form of unresolved questions. Foremost among them, perhaps, is, why, when Gold was willing to stoop to anything for his much-coveted government position, does it take another casual insult from his unpleasant father to make him decide to reject the call of the White House? One would have thought that any one of the false climaxes preceding this episode would have been sufficient: Gold's recognition of Kissinger's baseness and its relationship to his own, Gold's apparent heart-attack at the worst moment of his moral decay, the subsequent isolation, even the anti-Semitic abuse heaped upon him by Conover and the Governor. Furthermore, why should another insult from his father make him want to embrace the Jewishness he has been running away from for most of the rest of the book? Is it for the purely sentimental reason that, to paraphrase Gold, his brother is dead and his father is old? Sentiment has not been one of Gold's notable characteristics. It seems in some ways a curious reversal also that the Jews, who throughout most of the novel have been portrayed much as the stereotypes would have them—pushy, obnoxious, greedy; intellectual hypocrites and opportunists—should suddenly at the conclusion take on the sweet glow of appeal (indeed, as Gene Lyons, who reviewed *Good as Gold* for *The Nation*, pointed out, if anyone but a Jew had written this book, it would have been branded anti-Semitic).

One *could* find an answer in a remark of Heller's to one interviewer that Gold, like the author's other protagonists, is basically quite orthodox at heart. We have some confirmation of this assertion in Gold's moral outrage at Andrea's sexual proclivities and the freedom with which she practices and advertises them (with anyone but him), as well as in the universal presence of the agent Greenspan as Gold's Jewish conscience in the latter parts of the book. If "orthodoxy" in Heller's sense is to be taken also as a commitment to the faith of one's fathers, then Gold does indeed, like Yossarian, make a leap of faith at the end in the direction of traditional ideals, a leap of faith the reader is asked to make too. Apparently, although he has never been completely comfortable with his Jewishness, and in fact is an outsider among his own people, he ultimately prefers to embrace the ills he knows than to fly to others he knows less well.

It is true that the Jews become more attractive, even in their general contrariness, as the novel proceeds, particularly in contrast to what the WASP world offers. The most touching and human scenes of the book, of Heller's entire *oeuvre* in fact, are those in which Gold learns of the Jewish experience in America from his older siblings and acquaintances; this is not surprising when one learns that for these passages Heller borrowed heavily from the experiences of his own family. The question inevitably arises at this point: to what extent then is *Good as Gold* about "the Jewish experience in America? Could we even read in Gold's desperate, self-aggrandizing grab at power—power imitative of the successful Kissinger's—a metaphor for the struggle for acceptance in Anglo-Saxon society: the apparent necessity of dealing with deeply ingrained anti-Semitism, of being forced to live the stereotypes in order to join in the American Dream, of selling out to succeed?

This interpretation would be arguable were it not that Heller himself, on more than one occasion, has maintained in reference to this novel that there is nothing unique about "the Jewish experience in America," that it is essentially identical to the Irish or Italian experience, and that in fact "an American with a Jewish background [is] not much different from Americans of Irish background or protestant backgrounds" (from an unpublished interview). To Heller, "the Jewish experience in America" is apparently just another of those phrases of little meaning that permeate the book or, as he said on *The Dick Cavett Show*, "a joke." Perhaps it was this that the author was emphasizing when he made Pugh Conover as mad and contrary as Gold's stepmother and father combined, or when he loaded down Conover's tables with a culinary bounty greater than, though reminiscent of, that at the Gold family dinners. But except for a couple of fleeting references to the immigrants of other nationalities in the Coney Island area, Heller makes no obvious effort to draw the parallels he insists are there. Despite his own stated intentions, he makes the Jewish experience uniquely, and even stereotypically, Jewish.

That leaves the rest of the novel's matter, its political satire. We view the political system primarily by way of a few foci: Ralph Newsome, the Governor and his Commission, the Conovers, and, of course, Kissinger. Ralph—it has already been noted—is characterized by his tendency to contradict everything he says and to take seriously every remark Gold makes, no matter how casual or ironic. In this, Newsome emulates the mindlessness of the President, who spends his days in his office working on his memoirs. The Governor never comes across as anything but patronizing and heavy-handed, while the Commission he heads is a collection of virtually nameless grotesques concerned only with amassing their expense accounts, for which they do absolutely nothing.

All of the above-mentioned characters are cartoon figures, without depth or humanity. It may have been Heller's intent, in fact, to compare the politicians of the Seventies to creatures of low comedy. If so, this satire shoots very wide, as with birdshot, aiming broadly at politics as an institution rather than at particular practices of the near past or the present. Even if one compares the Governor or the President with well-known political contemporaries, one finds that the only point of the satire—that our politicians are in general too stupid or selfish to accomplish anything—falls short of the enormity of the sins of the Watergate era. Only when Heller deals with Kissinger and in passing other living personalities does he approach the truth. The Conovers are only tangentially involved in the political realm of the book; but likewise, they are one-dimensional, Conover being notable chiefly for his insanity, Andrea for her simple-minded degeneracy. As *The New Yorker* accurately observed, "The depravity of his characters is not spun of ingeniously twisted logic; it is too plain to be evil or funny . . . " (16 April 1979, p. 158).

On the other hand, Heller's commentary on Kissinger is extremely pointed. Most of it has been examined already: the universal dislike of the former Secretary among all classes and groups across the novel's spectrum, the frequent use of journalistic reports and widely circulated jokes against him, and so on, building up to the long tirade near the climax. As at least one reviewer wondered, however, can a collection of newspaper clippings be regarded as "satire"? If the rest of the political humor in the work is too broad and unfocused, that directed against Kissinger is so factual and specific as to overshoot the comic exaggeration characteristic of satire. It is as though Heller was balancing the general haziness of the one half of the political message against the stark specificity of the other.

Again, it could be argued that Heller, with his demonstrated talent for making rhetorical technique set up the framework for his themes, intended the *reality* of

Kissinger to burlesque itself; certainly most of the newspaper quotations have the unreal air of exaggeration, true though they may be. If nothing else they reveal the difficulties of dealing with facts and factual personalities that are stranger than fiction, as the author intimates through Gold during the Kissinger diatribe with the line, "In a novel no one would believe it." One might be reluctant to give the author this much credit in this case, however, considering the relatively random effects of the rest of the work. True, the repetition and contradiction characteristic of Heller are present, if only in the unsubtle forms used by Ralph and Gold's parents. In contrast to the carefully structured "free association" of the earlier novels, *Gold* flows with a sort of jumpy consistency, on the whole chronologically. There are a couple of glaring artistic anomalies in the work, however, of dubious rhetorical intent.

Perhaps the most striking is the author's sudden intervention and destruction of the fictive world in the passage that begins,

> Once again Gold found himself preparing to lunch with someone—Spotty Weinrock—and the thought arose that he was spending an awful lot of time in this book eating and talking. There was not much else to be done with him. I *was* putting him into bed a lot with Andrea and keeping his wife and children conveniently in the background. (p. 336)

He goes on in the paragraph to describe a number of complications he had considered for the plot, such as the hectic weekend in Acapulco that ends up in Gold's reveries. This is the only time the author intervenes in this fashion. Another one-shot effect is the coincidence of having Pugh Conover reminisce about a woman whom the reader immediately recognizes as Gold's stepmother. Gold, however, does not pick up the connection. Two pages later, Charles Dickens is invoked and described by Gold as "a long winded novelist . . . whose ponderous works were always too long and always flawed by a procession of eccentric, one-sided characters too large in number to keep track of, and an excessive abundance of extravagant coincidences and other unlikely events" (p. 411). This is clearly a coy reference to *Good as Gold* itself, which Heller has called in other contexts a Dickensian novel. As he has also said, "I wanted to get a sense in *Good as Gold* all the way through that it is not to be taken seriously as really having happened" (from an unpublished interview). By way of comparison, it is interesting to note that in his 1962 interview for *The Realist* (cited above), Heller insisted that *Catch-22* was *not* to be taken as a hallucination but as literally happening. This difference in approach reflects Heller's difference in purpose; while *Catch-22* purports to be a serious work of literature, *Good as Gold*, as one reviewer remarked borrowing the Yiddish *patois* of the novel, "is to laugh out loud" (*Library Journal*, 15 March 1979, p. 752).

Unfortunately, even as a work of straight humor it is not, despite *People* magazine, "far funnier than *Catch-22*," though it does have a number of very funny moments. Especially laughable is the detestable if harmless Lieberman, his own worst enemy, and the practical jokes played by Murray Weinrock at Gold's expense. And, of course, the prose is permeated with Heller's typical wit and irony. But the laughs in *Good as Gold* not only lack the variety and intent of those in *Catch-22*, they simply do not come as frequently.

Good as Gold is, in its way, more entertaining than *Something Happened*; and the humanity of the Jewish characters surrounding Gold, if not entirely full-fleshed, at least represents an interesting departure for Heller. But taking into account the relative carelessness and randomness of the author's effects and the questionable seriousness of purpose, *Good as Gold* must be considered Heller's weakest novel, without the depth, direction, or intensity of the other two.

V: CONCLUSION

The blessing of *Catch-22*'s critical and popular success has not been unmixed. Although the reputation of that novel made it easier for Heller's later works to reach a wide audience, each has had to stand up to the inevitable comparisons with the original masterpiece. To the author's credit, he has resisted the natural temptation to write *Catch-23* and *Catch-24*, unless one regards the plays as such. Instead, he has carried his imagination into very different battlefields, experimenting with other settings, moods, and methods. Nevertheless, there are a number of themes, motifs, techniques, and even flaws that run throughout his work.

Most of the flaws and alleged flaws have already been mentioned; some, like the one-dimensionality of many of Heller's characters and the use of redundancy, have been shown, in this study and elsewhere, to have thematic significance. Other problems, however, deserve attention at this point. One is the oft-criticized suddenness of Heller's climaxes, often leaving the reader unprepared and confused. In *Catch-22*, it was the news of Orr's reaching Sweden that brought a last-minute beam of hope into the dark world of the novel. In *Something Happened*, it was the fleeting episode of the accident and the smothering of Slocum's son. In *Good as Gold*, Sid's unexpected heart attack yanks Gold out of the world of politics. Even in the play *We Bombed in New Haven*, it is the sudden appearance of Starkey's son, heretofore unmentioned, that brings to a head the issues of the work. As we have seen, in *Catch-22* and *Something Happened* at least the climaxes *have* been prepared for, if subtly. Upon closer analysis, in addition, one does note a definite pattern in all of them. Their most striking similarity, other than their suddenness, is that each is brought about by forces external to the protagonist, by a *deus ex machina*, so to speak. Granted, both Slocum and Starkey ultimately hold the responsibility for the deaths of their respective sons, but in each case it was something beyond the character's control that created the situation in which he was forced to act—the war, the accident, etc.

It is worth noting as well that each of these climaxes is related to the sudden death of someone close to the protagonist. In *Catch-22*, although Snowden's death is the one prefigured as the cause for Yossarian's disillusionment with the war, it is the senseless death of his friend Nately that actually prompts him to reject it altogether. Captain Starkey does not formally acknowledge the cowardice that keeps him a member of the power structure until the death of his son. Slocum, of course, achieves his identification with power by killing his son, after which he is finally able to "take command." And Gold's decision to reject Washington comes at the funeral of his brother Sid. Curiously, this perpetual collocation was inadvertent on Heller's part; in his February 1980 interview with Dick Cavett, he confessed that he was only made aware of it after the publication of *Good as Gold*. The fact of death at his climaxes is thus not a conscious effect but derives automatically from the laws of Heller's fictive universe. What could it mean?

First of all, sudden, unexpected death does appear frequently in all the above-considered works. Clearly, death hovers center-stage in *Catch-22* and *We Bombed in New Haven*, often as a reminder of the worst price the system can extract from those trapped in it. Mortality makes its presence felt in subtler ways in the other novels. It pervades Slocum's morose consciousness, with his oft-repeated fears for the safety of himself, his vulnerable son, and reckless daughter. Periodically he recalls fatal events that have taken place around New York: a man shot to death in the park for no apparent reason, another killed in a grotesque subway accident. At one point in the narrative, Slocum sees a healthy-looking middle-aged man drop dead directly in front of him in the lobby of the building where he works. In *Good as Gold* a man also drops dead in the vicinity of the protagonist, this time in the gymnasium just before Gold's apparent heart attack. Death in *Gold*, however, is taken as a whole more lightly, true to the generally lighter spirit of the book—for example, the scene in which Gold's father and stepmother sit in front of the television identifying deceased actors in old movies.

Certainly, mortality is treated in all these works as the consummate force beyond one's control. Remembering the role it played in *Catch-22*, as the cosmic injustice of injustices, perhaps one could view death in Heller's world as the ultimate enemy, the final irony of an Absurd universe. One could stretch the point and suggest that only by confronting and in some sense mastering the fact of this ultimate tragic absurdity can one then become—or attempt to become—master of his own life. This conclusion would be consistent with the tenets of modern existentialism.

Of course, all of Heller's protagonists attempt to "take command" in different ways. There is more to the choices they must make than the simple assertion of self amid overwhelming external forces. In each of the novels, and less so in the plays, the protagonist is offered relatively early a set of ethical alternatives; the work then proceeds to examine all the ramifications of these alternatives up to the climactic point where a personal crisis triggers the protagonist's decision to opt for one code of values over the others, a decision that turns out to be not only desperate but irreversible. Yossarian, confronting a world at war being run by Scheisskopfs and Peckems, dominated by the values of Minderbinders and Cathcarts, chooses to disobey, to refuse his support of the system. Starkey, facing virtually an identical choice, opts in another direction. Slocum, offered the opportunity to join the ranks of the amoral but potent, likewise ultimately manages to suppress his individual humanity, what there is of it, in favor of the ruthless but efficacious code by which society operates. Gold is also strongly tempted by the opportunity to join on the side of unethical power, but is pulled back at the last moment by his apparently ingrained orthodoxy.

Other motifs in these works point up the same problem of trying to live as a moral individual in an immoral world and as a coherent individual in an absurd universe. One such motif is the oft-mentioned decay of society, which prompts each of the protagonists of the novels to long disquisitions (see, for instance, *Catch-22*, pp. 421-422; *Something Happened*, p. 454; *Good as Gold*, pp. 355-356). Another is the repeated presence of madness: the wholly insane world of

Catch-22, the more subtle incipient breakdowns of Martha, Holloway, and perhaps Slocum himself in *Something Happened*, the eccentric characters of *Good as Gold*. That much of the irrationality rests on paradoxes and contradictions exemplifies the difficulty of reconciling opposing but often equally strong ethical dicta: conscience vs. loyalty, love vs. obedience, compassion vs. security, integrity vs. success. Like the motif of social decay, madness thus suggests the moral chaos, the instability, of modern life, and even, like death, the fragility of the human spirit in the face of it. Heller, incidentally, comes down on the side of conscience, love, compassion, and integrity (though, as in the cases of Slocum and Gold, we are not always sure how the author regards his characters, which many critics have considered a weakness). As all these qualities have proven all but useless in the given contexts, Heller's ethical choice itself is, ironically or perhaps "logically," the Absurd one. Heller appears to be suggesting that virtue, in the form of personal integrity, is its own reward; he thus shows himself to be, despite the pessimistic, cynical vision he delineates in his work, a moral idealist at heart.

Heller, upon being asked which of his novels he considers the most worthy of relegating to posterity, has chosen *Something Happened* as "the most important book." He cites the temporality of the war issue and the political issue as grounds for the impermanence of *Catch-22* and *Good as Gold*. *Something Happened*, on the other hand, deals with the more intimate and, he believes, universal subject of one man's most personal relationships. He is probably right about *Good as Gold*, but the majority of Heller's fans will disagree, I am certain, with the rest. *Catch-22* remains Heller's most widely read and appreciated book; as long as there are institutions of any sort, and wars popular or unpopular, and ruthless ambition, ethical conflicts, and stupidity in high places, there should be an audience for *Catch-22*. *Something Happened* may have some appeal to the modern-day student of Heller, but the book is too ponderous and self-consciously literary to survive for long. *Good as Gold*, by contrast, is too light and tied, like the plays, to contemporary circumstances.

Where will Heller head next? He announced on his above-cited interview with Dick Cavett that he is considering a novel which would be narrated by the biblical King David, from the standpoint, however, of today. It would undoubtedly dip even deeper into Heller's Jewish heritage, despite the suggestion of reviewer Gene Lyons that Heller leave the Jews to Philip Roth and Woody Allen. It would also apparently combine the first-person technique of *Something Happened* with the humor of the other works. As of this writing, however, no work in progress has been seen, and it may be some years, given Heller's artistic habits, before the public gets a glimpse of his next novel. Whatever it turns out to be, we can probably expect Heller to push out in yet another new direction, while preserving the same basic theme of moral and ethical struggle in the face of the mortality, insanity, and absurdity of the human condition. Let us hope that he finally proves himself capable of writing books better than, or even as good as, his first and most famous creation.

BIBLIOGRAPHICAL NOTES

I. Works by Joseph Heller treated at length herein:
  Catch-22. New York: Simon and Schuster, 1961; New York: Dell, 1962; New York; Delta, 1964; New York: Modern Library, 1966; New York: Simon and Schuster, 1969 (Large type edition); New York: Clarion, 1969 (Large type edition); New York: Delta, 1973 (Critical edition).
  Catch-22: a Dramatization. New York: Samuel French, 1971 (Acting version); New York: Delacorte, 1973; New York: Delta, 1973 (With author's preface.)
  Good as Gold. New York: Simon & Schuster, 1979; New York: Pocket Books, 1979.
  Something Happened. New York: Knopf, 1974; New York: Ballantine, 1975.
  We Bombed in New Haven. New York: Delta, 1969; New York: Dell, 1970.
II. Works about Joseph Heller: A complete bibliography of books, articles, reviews, etc., that deal with Heller and his work would require another volume the length of this one. Worth mentioning, however, are the materials to which I am indebted for critical suggestions and quotations.

  a) Most helpful in connection with the chapter on *Catch-22* was *A Catch-22 Casebook*, edited by Frederick Kiley and Walter McDonald (New York: Crowell, 1973); of the many essays, interviews, and reviews it contains, I relied most on the following, some of which have already been cited in the text:

Gaukroger, Doug, "Time Structure in *Catch-22*," pp. 132-144.
MacDonald, James L. " 'I See Everything Twice!'; the Structure of Joseph Heller's *Catch-22*," pp. 102-108.
Mellard, James M. "*Catch-22*: Deja vu and the Labyrinth of Memory," pp. 109-121.
Milne, Victor J. "Heller's 'Bologniad': A Theological Perspective on *Catch-22*," pp. 58-73.
Protherough, Robert, "The Sanity of *Catch-22*," pp. 201-212.
Ritter, Jesse. "Fearful Comedy: *Catch-22* as Avatar of the Social Surrealist Novel," pp. 73-86.
Solomon, Jan. "The Structure of Joseph Heller's *Catch-22*," pp. 122-132.
Stark, Howard J. "The Anatomy of *Catch-22*," pp. 145-158.
  The interested reader is also encouraged to look at the collections cited below:
Nagel, James, ed. *Critical Essays on* Catch-22. California: Dickenson, 1974.
Scotto, Robert M., ed. *A Critical Edition of* Catch-22. New York: Delta, 1973.
  The most comprehensive bibliography of *Catch-22* is Joseph Weixlmann's "A Bibliography of Joseph Heller's *Catch-22*," *Bulletin of Bibliography*, 31/1 (Jan/March 1974), pp. 32-37.

  b) For the later work of Heller's up through *Something Happened*, a useful text is Robert M. Scotto's *Three Contemporary Novelists: An Annotated Bibliography of Works by and about John Hawkes, Joseph Heller, and Thomas Pynchon* (New York: Garland, 1977). Since relatively little criticism exists concerning the later works, I have had to rely mainly on reviews and interviews to supplement my arguments. In this regard I wish to thank at this point Martin Gardella of San Diego State University for giving me a copy of an unpublished interview with Joseph Heller he conducted in La Jolla, California, on March 29, 1980.